T0146360

INDIVIDUAL DIFFERENCES IN RESISTANCE TO TRUTH DECAY

Exploring the Role of Reasoning and Cognitive Biases

LUKE J. MATTHEWS ❙ ANDREW M. PARKER ❙ KATHERINE GRACE CARMAN
ROSE KERBER ❙ JENNIFER KAVANAGH

For more information on this publication, visit **www.rand.org/t/RRA112-17**.

About RAND

The RAND Corporation is a research organization that develops solutions to public policy challenges to help make communities throughout the world safer and more secure, healthier and more prosperous. RAND is nonprofit, nonpartisan, and committed to the public interest. To learn more about RAND, visit www.rand.org.

Research Integrity

Our mission to help improve policy and decisionmaking through research and analysis is enabled through our core values of quality and objectivity and our unwavering commitment to the highest level of integrity and ethical behavior. To help ensure our research and analysis are rigorous, objective, and nonpartisan, we subject our research publications to a robust and exacting quality-assurance process; avoid both the appearance and reality of financial and other conflicts of interest through staff training, project screening, and a policy of mandatory disclosure; and pursue transparency in our research engagements through our commitment to the open publication of our research findings and recommendations, disclosure of the source of funding of published research, and policies to ensure intellectual independence. For more information, visit www.rand.org/about/principles.

RAND's publications do not necessarily reflect the opinions of its research clients and sponsors.

About This Report

The concept of Truth Decay was introduced by Kavanagh and Rich (2018) and defined according to four societal trends: heightened disagreement about facts and analytical interpretations of facts and data, blurring of the line between opinion and fact, an increase in the relative volume and influence of opinion and personal experience over fact, and diminished trust in formerly respected institutions as sources of factual information.

In this report, we examine a proposed driver of this societal phenomenon: characteristics of human cognitive processing (such as cognitive biases). We conduct our examination within the context of social and demographic control variables. We describe our development of a survey measure to assess resistance/susceptibility to Truth Decay, and we discuss that quality's relationship with human cognitive processing.

The material in this report will be most useful to researchers interested in the measurement of resistance/susceptibility to Truth Decay or in the impact of cognitive biases. We present detailed data and statistical results, highlighting key findings and insights in the summary at the beginning of the report and in the concluding chapter.

This report is part of RAND's Countering Truth Decay initiative, which considers the diminishing role of facts and analysis in political and civil discourse and the policymaking process. The original report in the series, *Truth Decay: An Initial Exploration of the Diminishing Role of Facts and Analysis in American Public Life* by Jennifer Kavanagh and Michael D. Rich, was published in January 2018 and laid out a research agenda for studying and developing solutions to the Truth Decay challenge.

Funding

Funding for this research was provided by gifts from RAND supporters and income from operations.

Acknowledgments

We are grateful for the significant support we received along the way, without which this report would not have been possible. First, we would like to thank Michael D. Rich for his generous support, guidance, and feedback. We also thank David Grant, Karen Edwards, and Julie Newell for their excellent advice and assistance in developing and implementing the American Life Panel survey that provided this report with its data source and foundation. We thank C. Ben Gibson and David Kennedy of RAND and Keith Stanovich of the University of Toronto for their thoughtful reviews of our work. Thanks also to the many people who pilot tested the survey questions and provided encouragement along the way. All errors are the authors' own.

Summary

Truth Decay, as defined by Kavanagh and Rich (2018), is a societal phenomenon indicated by four key sociocultural trends: heightened disagreement
about facts and analytical interpretations of facts and data, blurring of the
line between opinion and fact, an increase in the relative volume and influence of opinion and personal experience over fact, and diminished trust in
formerly respected institutions as sources of factual information.

In this report, we address one of Truth Decay's proposed drivers: characteristics of human cognitive processing, such as cognitive biases. We first
sought to operationalize the idea of Truth Decay into a set of survey questions that would result in a quantitative measure of individuals' resistance
or susceptibility (considered the end points of a spectrum and hereafter
referred to as resistance/susceptibility) to Truth Decay. This establishment
of a quantitative measure is a common step in much of science and social
science. *Operationalizing* an idea means to render it measurable through
a concrete observational or experimental procedure, and this is an initial
step in scientific investigation that must occur before the causes of the phenomenon of interest can be studied. The scientist must have a concrete way
of observing the phenomenon (in this case, Truth Decay), and that usually
involves some degree of quantification (Bernard, 2018, Chapter 2).

We operationalized Truth Decay at the individual level as a way of gaug-
ing how people interpret facts and data, their ability to perceive differences
between facts and opinions, and their trust in formerly respected institutions as sources of factual information. We then assessed how resistance/
susceptibility to Truth Decay relate to the various filters through which
individuals interpret information (such as reasoning processes and cognitive biases). We also examined how much these features affected resistance/
susceptibility to Truth Decay compared with effects of other sociodemographic features of U.S. society (for example, race or religion) that control
for sociocultural factors but that might not be connected to variations in
cognitive processes among individuals. Although our research interests
were focused on cognitive processes, we performed this additional layer of
sociodemographic analysis in recognition that most researchers in whole
disciplines of social science, such as sociology and anthropology, would be

skeptical that such a phenomenon as Truth Decay could be reducible to cognitive mechanisms rather than emergent phenomena of particular sociocultural histories.

The interpretation of information relies on human cognitive processes. Cognitive biases or limits in cognitive processing abilities could contribute to differences in the interpretation of facts and data and could make it harder for individuals to differentiate facts from opinions. This, in turn, could contribute to the erosion of trust in institutions that are sources of factual information. Psychological, anthropological, and behavioral economics literatures have identified countless biases and limits to humans' reasoning ability; in this work, we focus on one specific cognitive processing skill—cognitive reasoning—and the cognitive biases that are potentially likely to influence resistance/susceptibility to Truth Decay.

In this research, our team carefully assessed a comprehensive list of cognitive biases and reasoning processes previously discussed in the aforementioned literature to focus on those most likely to relate to Truth Decay and that could be easily measured in a survey. We then developed a new measure of resistance/susceptibility to Truth Decay and deployed it as a survey conducted in the RAND American Life Panel. Our goal was to gain a better understanding of the links between (1) cognitive biases and reasoning and (2) resistance/susceptibility to Truth Decay. The work reported here is an initial step and should be considered exploratory in nature. In particular, this is the first time resistance/susceptibility to Truth Decay has been operationalized at the individual level. Therefore, the results presented here should be used to motivate future refinements in both measurement and conceptualization.

Measuring Resistance/Susceptibility to Truth Decay

Our measures of resistance/susceptibility to Truth Decay considered different aspects of Truth Decay, as originally specified by Kavanagh and Rich (2018), to allow for the possibility that there was heterogeneity in how people respond to information. Whenever possible, we employed previously published sets of survey questions (from authors other than Kavanagh and Rich) that addressed aspects of Truth Decay that corresponded to Kavanagh and Rich's conceptualization of the phenomenon (Kavanagh and Rich did not publish survey questions). For a few cases in which we could not find any previously published survey question sets, we devised our own questions that can rightly be regarded as more exploratory. We then used the full combined question set as our final survey instrument to operationalize individual-level variation in Truth Decay. In our approach, we considered the following six a priori (that is, based on deduction from theory rather than induced from the data) scales of resistance/susceptibility to Truth Decay:

- **Endorsement of scientific consensus.** We included six questions about information that scientists generally agree on as fact. Those who endorse such facts would be considered more resistant to Truth Decay. These questions were derived from Drummond and Fischhoff (2017) and Lewandowsky, Gignac, and Oberauer (2013), who had previously developed these particular six questions as valid indicators of endorsement of generally agreed-on scientific information.
- **Endorsement of verifiable facts.** We asked five questions about verifiable facts pertaining to events that have been reported in the news. Those who endorse such facts generally would be considered less susceptible to Truth Decay. We were unable to find a previously published set of verifiable journalistic fact questions, so we devised these ourselves.
- **Rejection of false conspiracy theories.** We asked five questions about belief in conspiracy theories. Conspiracy theories take many forms and are common across the political spectrum. Those who reject false conspiracy theories would be considered less susceptible to Truth Decay. These questions were similar to those used previously by Lewandowsky, Gignac, and Oberauer (2013) and Nowak et al. (2020). Gidengil et al. (2019) details results from a systematic literature review that informed the development of the questions used by Nowak et al. (2020).
- **Ability to distinguish fact from opinion.** Six questions focused on distinguishing between statements of fact and opinion—not whether a statement was true or false but whether it was factual in nature (and thus answerable from data) or an opinion (and thus only answerable by assuming some kind of value judgment). A blurring of the line between fact and opinion is one of the key trends defining Truth Decay. Those who cannot distinguish factual information from opinion-based state-

ments would be considered more susceptible to Truth Decay. We used questions developed and validated by the Pew Research Center (Mitchell et al., 2018) for assessing ability to distinguish fact from opinion.

- **Willingness to accept expert recommendations.** Eight questions asked panelists to rate their trust of various classes of experts, such as scientists, doctors, and government officials, among others. Whereas distrust in specific experts or on specific topics might not itself indicate susceptibility to Truth Decay, a generalized diminished trust in formerly respected institutions as sources of factual information has been identified as another key trend defining Truth Decay. Those who are unwilling to accept expert recommendations would be considered more susceptible to Truth Decay. We adapted these questions from a similar set of questions used in repeated surveys as part of the Americas Barometer survey (Vanderbilt University, undated).
- **Philosophical positivism versus skepticism.** We asked two questions about overarching philosophical perspectives regarding the objectivity of truth, which itself might underlie or derive from the aforementioned trends. Individuals could, on one hand, maintain positive affirmations that knowledge processes generate truth (that is, correspondence of ideas to some external reality); or, on the other hand, they could be skeptical that knowledge systems can generate truth at all. Those who perceive an external standard of truth would be considered more resistant to Truth Decay. We were unable to find a published question set to assess philosophical positivism versus skepticism, so we developed these questions ourselves.

Cognitive Biases and Reasoning Processes Considered in Our Work

Cognitive biases can be defined as "ways in which a person's beliefs, attitudes, reasoning, or decisions can deviate from reality or strict rationality as a result of patterns and tendencies in human processing" (Kavanagh and Rich, 2018, p. 81; Haselton, Nettle, and Murray, 2016). Put differently, cognitive biases are "systematic and predictable errors" that result from "highly economical and usually efficient" heuristic reasoning (Tversky and Kahneman, 1974).[1] We focused on the following three cognitive biases, hypothesized to increase susceptibility to Truth Decay:

1. **Availability bias** (Tversky and Kahneman, 1974). Events that are easier to recall are also judged as more likely (the availability heuristic), which can cause likelihood judgments to be biased toward more-salient or more-memorable events. Ability to perceive risks more accurately might lead to greater resistance to Truth Decay.

2. **Unjustified confidence** (Parker and Stone, 2014). An updated conceptualization of the older idea of overconfidence, *this* is confidence in knowledge (or perceived knowledge) that is unrelated to actual knowledge. A lack of understanding of the extent of one's own knowledge has the potential to limit information-seeking and to increase rejection of expert judgment.

3. **Ingroup bias** (Inglehart and Baker, 2000; Newheiser et al., 2015; Wilkins-Laflamme, 2018). This refers to a set of interrelated tendencies to feel more warmly toward one's own cultural group (for example, as defined by language, religion, or nationality) and to prefer them as partners during social interactions. Biases in favor of one's own cultural group might cognitively motivate skewed interpretations of facts in evidence.

We also identified three reasoning processes that could be associated with susceptibility to Truth Decay. A *reasoning process* is a set of cognitive operations that work together according to a particular logic or domain of thought and that are more extensive in scope than a more singular bias, which could be inserted within many cognitive pathways. Reasoning processes that were implicated in Truth Decay included

- **numeracy**, or skill with numbers, which has been shown to be a pervasive predictor of a wide variety of biases and decisionmaking behavior (Peters, 2020; Weller et al., 2013)

---

[1] A fallacy that often creeps into writing about these topics is that biases are adaptive; actually, the underlying heuristics are presumed to be adaptive.

- **scientific reasoning**, which extends the older concept of science literacy and has recently been identified as a potential driver of behaviors rejecting scientific consensus (for example, rejecting climate change and vaccine safety) (Drummond and Fischhoff, 2017; Drummond and Fischhoff, 2019)
- **magical reasoning**, which includes a variety of superstitious beliefs (Rosengren and French, 2013) and at least conceptually represents a counterpoint to logical and scientific reasoning.

Drawing on this logic, we hypothesized that greater numeracy and scientific reasoning skill will be associated with greater resistance to Truth Decay, whereas greater magical reasoning will be associated with greater susceptibility to Truth Decay.

Research Methods

For this work, we conducted a survey using the RAND American Life Panel (ALP). The ALP is a nationally representative panel that the RAND Corporation has used since 2006 to track individual attitudes toward a variety of political and other issues. Panel members are recruited to the ALP using probability-based sampling methods. Panel members agree to respond to regular online surveys, typically two to three per month. To ensure the representativeness of the panel, recruited individuals who did not previously have access to the internet were provided with a netbook computer and internet access. For this study, 1,333 panel members completed the survey, which was fielded from February 26 through March 13, 2019.

To test our main hypothesis that resistance to Truth Decay is associated with more rigorous reasoning and less cognitive bias, we first assessed bivariate correlations between cognitive measures and the measures of resistance/susceptibility to Truth Decay. We then conducted three sets of regression analyses:

- The first set predicts each of our proposed measures of resistance/susceptibility to Truth Decay by using our measures of reasoning and bias, both without and while controlling for a variety of sociodemographic covariates.

- The second set uses principal component analysis (PCA) to analyze responses to the Truth Decay questions in a manner agnostic to our own grouping of survey items. These component scores are then treated, similar to the six a priori scales of resistance/susceptibility to Truth Decay, as outcome variables in regression models with reasoning, biases, and our covariates as predictors. Because these component scores are data driven and involve many more items, the scores are also more reliable than the predefined measures.
- The third set uses cultural consensus analysis to analyze the data in a manner agnostic to definitions of truth. Instead, this method examines *consensus truth* (multivariate agreement among the sample) and how much an individual's beliefs deviate from the consensus. We then use the loadings of individuals on the consensus truth axis, similar to the aforementioned scales, as outcome variables in regression models with reasoning, biases, and our covariates as predictors.

Results

The proposed measures of resistance/susceptibility to Truth Decay were substantially and positively correlated with each other, consistent with there being a common underlying construct. Generally speaking, greater resistance to Truth Decay on each of the six scales was predicted by greater numeracy, greater scientific reasoning, and less magical reasoning, consistent with our primary hypothesis. Among the cognitive biases, greater availability bias was associated with greater susceptibility to false conspiracy theories but also with greater willingness to accept expert recommendations. Counter to expectations, greater unjustified confidence by individuals in their own knowledge was associated with greater willingness to accept expert recommendations. Ingroup bias was at times associated with greater susceptibility to Truth Decay (lower endorsement of scientific consensus and verifiable fact, lower philosophical positivism) and at other times associated with greater resistance to Truth Decay (rejection of false conspiracy theories, ability to distinguish fact from opinion). In terms of demographics, resistance to Truth Decay indicators was most consistently associated with those who had a higher income, those who were White, and those who voted for Hillary Clinton in 2016.

Recognizing the exploratory nature of this initial study and that our six Truth Decay scales reflect our own assumptions of how the separate Truth Decay questions are interrelated, we also submitted the 33 individual Truth Decay–related survey questions to a PCA. This method of analysis combines survey items on scales using only the observed patterns of covariation among them. This analysis detected three substantial components describing the variability in the items. The first component corresponded to endorsement of scientific consensus, rejection of false conspiracy theories, and willingness to accept recommendations or information from experts. This component also had somewhat weaker positive associations with endorsement of verifiable fact and ability to distinguish fact from opinion. Hence, this first component corresponds most closely to what we a priori considered to be overall resistance to Truth Decay. Resistance to Truth Decay on this dimension was associated with greater numerical and scientific reasoning and lower magical reasoning—and, when controlled for, was associated with having a higher income, identifying as White, voting for Clinton in 2016, and being less religious.

The second component captured respondents who showed some ability to distinguish fact from opinion but were skeptical rather than trusting of experts. Individuals who score high on this dimension of Truth Decay generally disbelieve conspiracy theories and consistently endorse some scientific consensus and verifiable fact items. Considered all together, this component appears to measure agreement or disagreement with a truth-informed political conservatism that is yet highly distrustful of societal experts. Individuals with more resistance to Truth Decay on this dimension tend to have greater scientific reasoning and less availability bias and less magical reasoning, but they also have greater ingroup bias. When sociodemographic variables are controlled for, those with greater resistance to Truth Decay tended to be above age 50 and to identify as White or Asian, politically Republican or independent, and nonreligious or not particularly religious.

The third component reflects politically partisan positions on the issues, and we consider respondents at either end of the political spectrum to have a high susceptibility to Truth Decay. For this third component, people at one end of this spectrum are labeled *conservative partisans* (with such characteristics as trusting business and religious leaders most, rejecting 9/11 trutherism, endorsing Obama birtherism,[2] rejecting evolution, and believing that genetically modified food is safe). Those at the other end of this component, in contrast, are labeled *liberal partisans* (with such characteristics as trusting scientists and distrusting business and religious leaders, endorsing 9/11 trutherism, rejecting Obama birtherism, endorsing evolution, and believing that genetically modified food is unsafe). Consistent with this interpretation, the most important demographic associations are with religious affiliation (evangelical on the conservative end, no religion or atheist/agnostic on the liberal end), religious service attendance, political party, and reported 2016 presidential voting for Clinton or Trump. Also consistent with this interpretation that both ends of this component equally reflect a high susceptibility to Truth Decay (but alternative partisan versions of it), the reasoning and bias measures are not especially associated with either end of the scale.

Finally, we conducted a Cultural Consensus Analysis (CCA) to provide a further robustness check on these interpretations. This analysis relaxes the assumption of an external scholarly standard for truth and instead defines the term merely as the consensus view among the respondents, leaving external scholarly standards out of the equation. This analysis largely replicates the previous analysis but with some loss of significance for some variables. Among the biases and reasoning measures, greater ingroup bias and greater unjustified confidence are both significantly associated with resistance to Truth Decay in the regression with consensus truth as the outcome; numeracy, scientific reasoning, and magical reasoning all lose significance. The loss of significance for some predictor variables could arise merely from the loss of information in the consensus method. In this method, the CCA eliminates information about which end of the spectrum of responses for each survey item is true based on scholarly consensus. Rather, the agreement of the majority of respondents across the main dimension of responses is induced by CCA to be the "truth." It is notable, however, that the items that

---

[2] *Trutherism* refers to the theory that the U.S. government, government agencies, or individuals within such agencies were either responsible for or purposefully complicit in the attacks of September 11, 2001 (9/11). *Birtherism* refers to the theory that Barack Obama was born outside the United States and thus not a "natural born citizen" as the U.S. Constitution stipulates is required to serve as president.

retain significant associations with *resistance* to Truth Decay (ingroup bias and unjustified confidence) are ones that seem implicitly linked to greater ethnocentrism. Anthropologists have long contended that ethnocentrism is a normal psychosocial state across individuals in nearly all societies studied (Langness, 1987). Regarding demographics, in the CCA, respondents whose views are most consistent with the cultural consensus truth tend to identify as White, vote Democratic, and report higher household incomes; we observed no significant associations with education, gender, age, or religious affiliation and observance.

Discussion

As far as we know, this is the first study to conduct a comprehensive assessment of resistance/susceptibility to Truth Decay correlated with variations among individuals. The six-category survey instrument addresses three of the four trends defining Truth Decay (Kavanagh and Rich, 2018), providing a multifaceted view that can be examined using its individual scales (as we did in our first set of regressions) or more holistically (as in our second and third sets of regressions). Although a promising proof of concept, this is the first test of this instrument, which will clearly benefit from further testing and refinement to ensure that it is reliable, valid, and free of any bias.

The most consistent finding across models was that greater numerical and scientific reasoning and lower magical reasoning were associated with greater resistance to Truth Decay. We did not find strong or consistent associations between resistance/susceptibility to Truth Decay and well-known cognitive biases (for example, availability bias, unjustified confidence). Rather, the greatest predictors we found for resistance/susceptibility to Truth Decay were reasoning processes that are developed over an individual's lifetime and are all at least somewhat adaptive within their proper context. This suggests that potentially powerful tools to combat Truth Decay might reside within the educational system (conceived broadly) rather than in attempts to counter biases related to "fast thinking" cognitive heuristics (Kahneman, 2011). Society needs to be better at developing informed and critically thinking citizens who can appropriately process the rapid media environments in which information consumers must now operate.

We note that we were unable to assess several biases that simply were not amenable to brief survey instruments; these are important questions for further study. We particularly want to note that we did not include myside bias (closely associated with confirmation bias and motivated reasoning) among the biases we measured because it was not amenable to measurement through a brief set of survey items. Myside bias occurs when a committed belief induces a misinterpretation of evidence, as opposed to when a misinterpretation of evidence induces a belief. Given that demographics were quite predictive of resistance/susceptibility to Truth Decay, myside bias could account for some of the associations with demographics, so these results should be interpreted in light of this possibility. For example, we found that respondents who self-reported as Democrats and less religious were more likely to accept evolution as a fact than were respondents who self-reported as Republicans and more religious. That acceptance could occur through myside bias, which would mean that Republican and more-religious respondents adopt a belief against evolution for some reason *not having to do with interpretation of evidence* (perhaps simple cultural copying or identity signaling) and then misinterpret facts and evidence in order to maintain this belief. Other processes could also account for this association, however. For example, information about natural history (particularly information that provides compelling evidence of evolution) might be presented differently in the schools and homes of Republican and more-religious respondents—or it might not be presented at all. Having received less or no exposure to clear evidence for evolution, some of these respondents might logically disbelieve it. That causal pathway illustrates how resistance/susceptibility to Truth Decay could result from particular cultures' histories without the presence of any particular cognitive biases, such as myside bias.[3]

A concerning finding across our models was that self-reported non-White respondents were consistently more susceptible to Truth Decay. Although race was not always significant, it often was significant even after

---

[3] We did explore the potential of two other biases—framing effects and resistance to the law of small numbers—using single items. In the end, we did not have confidence in these assessments. Comprehensive assessments for framing, in particular, can be quite long (Bruine de Bruin, Parker, and Fischhoff, 2007), and therefore were beyond the resources of this study.

controlling for other variables, such as education, political party, and biases or reasoning processes. This finding potentially reflects distrust of traditional sources of factual information among groups that have, at times, been systematically persecuted by societal institutions of government, medicine, and science. The findings underscore the need for ongoing and open conversations about truth with all demographics in the United States.

This observation about self-reported non-White respondents has been noted in previous studies (Bogart et al., 2021; Uscinski and Parent, 2014; Westergaard et al., 2014), and might not be caused directly by any single cognitive process, such as myside bias. Non-White respondents are thought to be more disposed to believe conspiracy theories because they have at times been victims of actual well-documented conspiracies (for example, the Tuskegee syphilis experiments on Black men and the World War II internment of Japanese Americans). A similar process might occur with low-income, rural, White Americans (especially in the Southeast), who, in contrast to notions of the "American Dream," experience lower social mobility and consequently higher multigenerational poverty than seen in nearly any other developed country (Alesina, Glaeser, and Sacerdote, 2001; Reeves and Krause, 2018). Again, distrust of the establishment by members of a group maltreated by this establishment could be a rational reaction derived from observing that the establishment does not help them.

The empirical results of this study contradict interpretations that members of non-White racial groups have less resistance to Truth Decay as a result of cognitive differences between these groups and White ones. If this process were happening, then our models should have found no effect of race on resistance to Truth Decay after controlling for reasoning processes and cognitive biases, because the hypothesized process would be that racial differences in cognition drive the differences in resistance/susceptibility to Truth Decay. We did not find this result; instead, racial differences are frequently significant after controlling for observable variation in cognition. This suggests, once again, that different cultural histories within U.S. society might play a greater role in resistance to Truth Decay than do individual-level variations in reasoning processes or cognitive biases. Further research is needed to disentangle how the various cognitive, cultural, or historical processes account for the correlations we observed between resistance to Truth Decay and demographic variables.

Our models also highlight how perceptions of key issues, worldviews, and even ways of processing information in the United States are now split according to partisanship and religiosity. Controlling for these variables in a multiple regression model often eliminated the significance of many of the reasoning processes and biases seen in bivariate correlations. Assuming the cross-sectional regression is picking up on the most important variables, combating Truth Decay might be just as much a matter of somehow bridging the partisan politics of U.S. society as it is a matter of addressing cognitive processes.

If these results—that there is a substantial disconnect between generally accepted truth and certain sociodemographic and political groups—hold, a distrust of societal experts will make it difficult to identify any traditionally trusted category of messenger (for example, journalists, religious leaders) who would be credible to reestablish truth claims with all parts of the American public. This, in turn, would be a substantial barrier to identifying common factual grounds on which to generate widespread support for policy solutions. The results presented here are the first with a survey-based assessment of resistance/susceptibility to Truth Decay and suggest the value of further refinement and inquiry.

Contents

Figure and Tables

Figure

Tables

CHAPTER ONE

Introduction

The concept of Truth Decay, introduced by Kavanagh and Rich (2018), is defined according to four documented societal trends: heightened disagreement about facts and analytical interpretations of facts and data, blurring of the line between opinion and fact, an increase in the relative volume and influence of opinion and personal experience over fact, and diminished trust in formerly respected institutions as sources of factual information. Although Kavanagh and Rich documented these trends and hypothesized about their potential causes, the authors did not collect new data to test those hypotheses. In this report, we describe our efforts to operationalize a draft measure of resistance or susceptibility (considered opposite ends of a spectrum and hereafter referred to as resistance/susceptibility) to Truth Decay and proceed with a correlational analysis to examine one of Truth Decay's proposed drivers: characteristics of human cognitive processing, such as cognitive biases. Operationalization of ideas is an important concept in social science and in science generally. To *operationalize* an idea in science means to render it measurable through concrete observational or experimental procedures. This is an initial step in scientific investigation that must occur before the causes of the phenomenon of interest can be studied. The scientist must have a concrete way of observing the phenomenon (in this case, Truth Decay), and that usually involves some degree of quantification (Bernard, 2018, Chapter 2). How people interpret facts and data, their ability to perceive differences between facts and opinions, and their trust in formerly respected institutions as sources of factual information (key trends identified as part of Truth Decay) are likely to be related to how they process information, their worldview, and the biases that shape both. This research delves into the links among these concepts.

The trends identified by Kavanagh and Rich (2018) are society-wide. Table 1.1 provides examples of the four documented trends associated with

TABLE 1.1

The Four Trends of Truth Decay

Trend	Example
Increasing disagreement about facts and analytical interpretations of facts and data	The shift in opinion about the safety of vaccines and genetically modified food; public perception of trends in violent crime in the United States
A blurring of the line between opinion and fact	Journalistic pieces that do not distinguish clearly between opinion and fact (for example, "News Page Columns" in the *New York Times*)
The increasing relative volume, and resulting influence, of opinion and personal experience over fact	Speculation, opinion, and falsehoods disseminated in traditional media (for example, newspapers and television) and social media channels that drown out verifiable data (for example, on such topics as the effect of immigration on jobs and crime)
Declining trust in formerly respected sources of factual information	Significant drops in public confidence and trust in government, newspapers, television news, books, the judiciary, and the presidency, as indicated by polls

SOURCE: Kavanagh and Rich, 2018, Table S.1.

Truth Decay. Overall, we see these trends at the population level or in the national discourse.

Our measure of resistance/susceptibility to Truth Decay operationalizes these trends at an individual level. As an example, Kavanagh and Rich (2018) documents a blurring of the line between facts and opinions in the press and media. Our survey seeks to measure whether individual respondents are able to accurately distinguish factual claims (statements that can be adjudicated through observation or evidence) from opinion claims (statements that involve a value judgment). Whether these claims are accurate is unimportant—the only issue of concern for this analysis is whether the statement is based on opinions or on verifiable information that may or may not be true (that is to say, information that might be incorrect but is verifiable).

Truth Decay, as originally defined by Kavanagh and Rich, includes the declining role that facts and evidence play in how society talks or thinks about key issues. Cognitive processes (and biases in particular) are posited as one mechanism behind Truth Decay: People are often more likely to justify their beliefs by turning to opinion or anecdote than to facts and data that might be available. However, not all faulty reasoning leads to Truth Decay, and Truth Decay is not a result of simply faulty reasoning.

Truth Decay is a decline within public discourse of the use of facts and evidence and a relative increase in the use of opinion that is associated with a reduction in beliefs corresponding to the way things are. How people interpret facts and data, people's ability to differentiate between facts and opinions, and people's trust in formerly respected institutions as sources of factual information are likely to be strong indicators of how susceptible people are to these trends in society. Some individuals might be better able to understand facts and data; others might have a better sense of when statements rely on facts and when they are based in opinion. Lack of trust in respected institutions also might contribute to susceptibility to Truth Decay. In this report, we describe how we used these ideas to develop a new measure of resistance/susceptibility to Truth Decay. Our goal was to objectively measure whether individuals are more or less susceptible to each of these trends associated with Truth Decay.

Notably, Truth Decay is a phenomenon that has been observed in various forms in specific historical periods in U.S. society, including the present (Kavanagh and Rich, 2018). It is a phenomenon to explain, not an explanation itself. Because of its effects on political discourse and policymaking (and, by implication, the outcome of those policies), the Truth Decay phenomenon is of pressing importance to the survival of the republic.

Cognitive Biases and Their Role in Resistance/ Susceptibility to Truth Decay

How people interpret information and make decisions is fundamentally based in human cognitive systems, and limitations in those systems can lead to biased reasoning. These cognitive systems and limitations can influence how people interpret facts and opinions and how they conceive of and communicate truth. *Cognitive biases*, which affect all people and are not eliminated by education or training, can be defined as "ways in which a person's beliefs, attitudes, reasoning, or decisions can deviate from reality or strict rationality as a result of patterns and tendencies in human processing" (Kavanagh and Rich, 2018, p. 81; also see Haselton, Nettle, and

Murray, 2016). Put differently, cognitive biases are "systematic and predictable errors" that result from "highly economical and usually efficient" heuristic reasoning (Tversky and Kahneman, 1974, p. 1131).[1]

There are many types of cognitive bias. These biases can stem from limitations in basic cognitive processes (for example, memory recall errors) or complex reasoning (for example, limited skill at using numbers); they also might have motivational origins (that is, *motivated reasoning*; see Kahne and Bowyer, 2018; and Scheufele and Krause, 2019) or stem from confirmatory biases (that is, *myside bias*; see Stanovich, West, and Toplak, 2013). Diverse processes might underpin motivation-based biases, but the tendency to prefer information consistent with prior beliefs (confirmation bias) and the tendency to prefer one's own sociocultural group to others (ingroup bias or ethnocentrism) both might manifest as motivated reasoning. Cognitive biases also include tendencies to perceive events as more likely when instances are easier to recall (Tversky and Kahneman, 1974) and to react differently to risky choices depending on whether consequences are framed in terms of gains or losses (Levin, Schneider, and Gaeth, 1998). They can involve excessive confidence in one's own knowledge (Alba and Hutchinson, 2000), even when those beliefs are false or based on misleading information (Parker and Stone, 2014), allowing false narratives to thrive and disinformation to survive and spread. Each of these biases and the many others that exist can affect how people interpret facts and data or how they differentiate between facts and opinions.

Cognitive biases can be quite difficult to overcome, partly because they rely on otherwise advantageous heuristics or other aspects inherent to human cognition (Kahneman, 2011). Humans regularly use these heuristics because typical decisions often do not warrant the time and effort required for more systematic processing. As a result, such heuristic processing is often automatic and hard to turn off (Kahneman, 2011; Reyna, 2008). That said, individuals vary in their tendency to rely on heuristic processing, and even individual reliance can vary depending on situation and context; thus, individuals also vary in their susceptibility to cognitive biases and the ease with which they overcome these ingrained biases (Bruine de Bruin,

---

[1] There is a fallacy that often creeps into writing about these topics that biases are adaptive, when it is actually the underlying heuristics that are presumed to be adaptive.

Parker, and Fischhoff, 2007; Stanovich, 2011; Stanovich and West, 2000). For some people, being confronted with facts that conflict with a preexisting belief only strengthens the preexisting belief (Nyhan et al., 2014; Opel et al., 2019). Others are more willing to change their minds but typically only when messages are communicated by trusted messengers and in specific contexts (Brunson and Sobo, 2017).

In addition to cognitive biases, *numeracy* (that is, skill with numbers) and scientific reasoning skills will likely shape how people think about facts that make use of numeric or scientific arguments. A growing literature has linked numeracy with a variety of cognitive biases (Nelson et al., 2008; Peters, 2020). Research extending science literacy to the ability to reason using scientific concepts has linked the latter with willingness to accept or reject scientific consensus (Drummond and Fischhoff, 2017; Drummond and Fischhoff, 2019). Conversely, magical reasoning could lead individuals to engage differently with facts and evidence because magical forms of thought, by definition, are predicated on causal interactions that defy a culture's conventional understandings of causality (Rosengren and French, 2013). Across many cultures, magical causation often involves supernatural contagion (for example, holy or evil people's bodies and possessions impart holiness or evil) or supernatural links by similarity (for example, similar alignment of stars at birth predicts similar behavioral traits). We hypothesized that magical reasoning might be linked to resistance/susceptibility to Truth Decay via a tendency to see connections between events that are not connected by conventional explanations. Prior research specifically on conspiracy theories supports the hypothesis that conspiratorial and magical beliefs are correlated because of underlying cognitive variations across people that influence both of these belief types (Brotherton and French, 2014).

To counter cognitive biases that contribute to the spread of disinformation (and, ultimately, to Truth Decay), there needs to be an understanding about which forms of cognitive bias are most relevant and the factors that drive them. Doing so requires review and prioritization of a wide variety of cognitive biases and related reasoning processes. It also requires development of instruments to systematically assess individual resistance/susceptibility to Truth Decay—a resource that had been lacking. Specifically, such an instrument should, to the extent possible, address the Truth

Decay trends we have described and examine how they interrelate and, in turn, relate to proposed indicators of reasoning and biases.

The promise of this exercise is a greater basis for understanding how to counter Truth Decay by either addressing the underlying cognitive drivers or altering the situations causing cognitive processes to go awry while not hindering mechanisms that function advantageously in other situations. **Specifically, the research presented here tests the hypothesis that more logical reasoning and less cognitive bias are associated with greater resistance to Truth Decay.** Testing this hypothesis helps create a foundation for developing interventions and extending the science to consider other issues, such as how social dynamics (for example, social media and social networks) can exacerbate cognitive biases and encourage the spread of disinformation and the formation of social echo chambers.

Objective and Outline of This Report

This report describes our initial exploratory attempts to operationalize Truth Decay at the individual level through a set of survey items and to examine how reasoning processes and cognitive biases might contribute to the sociocultural phenomenon of Truth Decay. We took a multimethod approach to this goal. In Chapter Two, we discuss how we developed indicators of individual resistance/susceptibility to Truth Decay using three of the four definitional trends offered by Kavanagh and Rich (2018). We then used an open-ended card-sort method to identify and prioritize reasoning processes and biases that could influence Truth Decay, which were operationalized into survey questions based on prior research, as described in Chapter Three. These measures were then fielded to a national sample of U.S. adults participating in the RAND American Life Panel (ALP), as described in Chapter Four. We present our results in Chapter Five and conclude with implications, limitations, and future directions in Chapter Six. The appendixes include the full set of survey questions, details about the resulting survey scale characteristics, and additional details about the analytic methods.

CHAPTER TWO

Identifying Indicators of Individual Resistance/Susceptibility to Truth Decay

To operationalize Truth Decay through a set of survey items, we examined how Kavanagh and Rich (2018) conceptualized Truth Decay as a sociocultural phenomenon that is more or less manifest at various points in U.S. history. Kavanagh and Rich (2018) identified four trends that make up Truth Decay:

1. increasing disagreement over basic facts and data
2. a blurring of the line between fact and opinion
3. expanding relative volume of opinion over fact
4. declining trust in formerly respected sources of factual information.

The third of these is a characteristic of the media environment in which individuals reside; as a result, we did not operationalize it at the individual level. Because our interest was in assessing individual differences in resistance/susceptibility to Truth Decay, we focused on identifying indicators for the other three trends (1, 2, and 4). In addition to operationalizing these three trends, we include two exploratory items assessing potential underlying philosophical perspectives on the nature of truth (philosophical positivism versus skepticism). We did this after the issue of modern forms of philosophical skepticism had been raised during presentations by Kavanagh of the original Truth Decay report as a potentially underexplored aspect of the Truth Decay phenomenon. The rest of this chapter describes the specific indicators. Verbatim question wording can be found in Appendix A. Additional detail and discussion of our methods is contained in Appendix C.

It is important to note that we intentionally did not confine the notion of factual information for this study to only scientific forms of evidence. U.S. society generally has recognized many other forms of fact and evidence that do not conform to the scientific method, which relies on the ability of individuals to independently observe, and thereby replicate or falsify, the empirical claims of other individuals. Truth Decay can apply to scientific facts, but it also can be a much broader phenomenon applicable to a variety of nonscientific topics. For example, a legal debate occurred within the U.S. Congress in 2021 as to whether a former president can be impeached after having left office. There are no scientific facts about this because it is not a question about repeatedly observable features of the world. However, U.S. society would generally agree that there are legal facts and evidence on this matter that can be ascertained through the methods of legal case law and constitutional interpretation that have existed since before the advent of modern science and have little to do with scientific thought processes. In what follows, we note when pertinent facts are more or less scientific in nature.

Increasing Disagreement over Basic Facts and Data

To operationalize this Truth Decay trend, we included three question sets in the survey fielded to the ALP. The first set consisted of six questions assessing individuals' ability to recognize and endorse scientific consensus (for example, safety of genetically modified food for human consumption). The second set, consisting of five questions, focused on verifiable facts from the news (for example, decreasing violent crime rates in the United States). The third set, consisting of five questions, addressed acceptance of conspiracy theories.

In our approach, we considered the following six a priori (that is, based on deduction from theory rather than induced from the data) scales of resistance/susceptibility to Truth Decay:

- **Endorsement of scientific consensus.** We included six questions about information that scientists generally agree on as fact. Those who endorse such facts would be considered more resistant to Truth Decay.

These questions were derived from Drummond and Fischhoff (2017) and Lewandowsky, Gignac, and Oberauer (2013), who had previously developed these particular six questions as valid indicators of endorsement of generally agreed-on scientific information.

- **Endorsement of verifiable facts.** We asked five questions about verifiable facts pertaining to events that have been reported in the news. Those who endorse such facts generally would be considered less susceptible to Truth Decay. We were unable to find a previously published set of verifiable journalistic fact questions, so we devised these ourselves.

- **Rejection of false conspiracy theories.** We asked five questions about belief in conspiracy theories. Conspiracy theories take many forms and are common across the political spectrum. Those who reject false conspiracy theories would be considered less susceptible to Truth Decay. These questions were similar to those used previously by Lewandowsky, Gignac, and Oberauer (2013) and Nowak et al. (2020). Gidengil et al. (2019) details results from a systematic literature review that informed the development of the questions used by Nowak et al. (2020).

- **Ability to distinguish fact from opinion.** Six questions focused on distinguishing between statements of fact and opinion—*not* whether a statement was true or false but whether it was factual in nature (and thus answerable from data) or an opinion (and thus only answerable by assuming some kind of value judgment). A blurring of the line between fact and opinion is one of the key trends defining Truth Decay. Those who cannot distinguish factual information from opinion-based statements would be considered more susceptible to Truth Decay. We used questions developed and validated by the Pew Research Center (Mitchell et al., 2018) for assessing ability to distinguish fact from opinion.

- **Willingness to accept expert recommendations.** Eight questions asked panelists to rate their trust of various classes of experts, such as scientists, doctors, and government officials, among others. Whereas distrust in specific experts or on specific topics might not itself indicate susceptibility to Truth Decay, a generalized diminished trust in formerly respected institutions as sources of factual information has been identified as another key trend defining Truth Decay. Those who are unwilling to accept expert recommendations would be considered more susceptible to Truth Decay. We adapted these questions from a similar set of questions used in repeated surveys as part of the AmericasBarometer survey (Vanderbilt University, undated).

- **Philosophical positivism versus skepticism.** We asked two questions about overarching philosophical perspectives regarding the objectivity of truth, which itself might underlie or derive from the aforementioned trends. Individuals could, on one hand, maintain positive affirmations that knowledge processes generate truth (that is, correspondence of ideas to some external reality); or, on the other hand, they could be skeptical that knowledge systems can generate truth at all. Those who perceive an external standard of truth would be considered more resistant to Truth Decay. We were unable to find a published question set to assess philosophical positivism versus skepticism, so we developed these questions ourselves.

Table 2.1 summarizes the question sets and other measures of resistance/susceptibility to Truth Decay used in our survey.

Respondents were asked to rate the likelihood that each of six statements for which there is broad scientific consensus was true (for example, "human activities have contributed to the recent rise in global temperature," or "homeopathic remedies are ineffective"). Responses were given on a five-point scale (for example, very likely to very unlikely), with one end being

TABLE 2.1

Measures of Resistance to Truth Decay

Measure	Source	Number of Items
Endorsement of scientific consensus	Drummond and Fischhoff, 2017; Lewandowsky, Gignac, and Oberauer, 2013	6
Endorsement of verifiable facts	Developed for this report	5
Rejection of false conspiracy theories	Gidengil et al., 2019; Nowak et al., 2020	5
Ability to distinguish fact from opinion	Mitchell et al., 2018	6
Willingness to accept expert recommendations	Vanderbilt University, undated	8
Philosophical positivism versus skepticism	Developed for this report	2

more in line with scientific consensus. Each response was scored as correct if the respondent selected one of the two response categories on that end ("likely" or "very likely" for statements that are true; "unlikely" or "very unlikely" for statements that are false). Overall scores were computed as the sum of correct answers, from 0 to 6.

Respondents were also asked about their perceptions regarding five topics for which factual information has been broadly presented in the news (for example, number of noncombatants killed by drone strikes).[1] Each question had three response options, one of which was consistent with facts reported in the news. A summary score was computed as the number of correct responses, from 0 to 5. We separated these conceptually from acceptance of scientific consensus because answers to some of these questions, although empirical in nature, are difficult to justify through proper scientific methods whereby independent observers verify or falsify claims. Many journalistic claims, although they report empirical facts, must obtain these facts via other forms of evidence, such as witness testimony or census records that are not replicable by other observers.

Drawing on prior work on vaccine policy, we posited that a related area of disagreement over basic facts and data involved rejection of false conspiracy theories. Building on a prior systematic literature review of all articles after 1999 with open-ended survey and interview responses about vaccines and conspiracies (Gidengil et al., 2019), and a study that compared anti-vaccine views from a nationally representative survey of more than 500 parents with tweets from tens of thousands of Twitter accounts (Nowak et al., 2020), we asked respondents the degree to which they agreed, ranging from strongly disagreed (0) to strongly agreed (5) with each of five false conspiracy theories (for example, "The US government caused or let the 9/11 attack happen on purpose").[2] An "unsure" option was also provided, to distinguish it from

---

[1] A sixth item on trends in numbers of immigrants entering the United States was found to be potentially misleading; indeed, such trends have reversed recently. Because of this, that item was excluded from analysis. This item is presented with the rest of the scale in Appendix A.

[2] *Trutherism* refers to the theory that the U.S. government, government agencies, or individuals within such agencies were either responsible for or purposefully complicit in the attacks of September 11, 2001 (9/11).

neither agree nor disagree. A summary score was computed as the average of all available responses and also ranged from 0 to 5.[3]

In part for consistency with prior psychological research (for example, Lewandowsky, Gignac, and Oberauer, 2013) we asked questions only about conspiracy theories generally agreed to be false. Stanovich, West, and Toplak (2016) similarly assesses rejection of conspiracy beliefs, although with a much longer scale.

We note that all the items discussed in this section should be regarded as self-reported in that it is possible the respondents could have different views than they reported on our survey. We know only what they reported to us. We designated these types of items throughout this report as *self-reported* to distinguish them from *performance items*, such as the numerical reasoning test. The performance nature of some items means that they do not present the same level of concern that respondents might report a belief or characteristic that is a misrepresentation or that does not match with what an objective outside observer might report. However, it is worth noting that individuals might apply themselves much less or more to a performance task in a survey than they would to that same performance task in their normal life.

Blurring the Line Between Fact and Opinion

We incorporated a recent, high-profile questionnaire by the Pew Research Center (Mitchell et al., 2018) that addressed the ability to distinguish statements based on verifiable fact from those relying on values or opinion. An example statement is, "Immigrants who are in the U.S. illegally have some rights under the Constitution." Respondents were not asked whether such statements were true or false, or whether there are facts in support of them, but instead asked to determine whether the statement could be verified through facts alone (fact statement) or relied at least in part on values and thus could not be verified through facts alone (opinion statement). Responses to six such statements were coded correct or incorrect depending on whether

---

[3] As described in more detail in Chapter Five, "unsure" responses were recoded as the mean of the responses for the related survey items for each individual. This is equivalent to taking the average of all non-"unsure" responses.

the respondent made the "correct" rhetorical determination, as had already been defined by the Pew Research Center. A summary score was computed as the sum of correct responses, from 0 to 6. We considered these items a performance assessment.

Declining Trust in Formerly Respected Sources of Factual Information

We asked eight questions through which we assessed respondents' willingness to accept the recommendations or information provided by experts when they are advising within their area of expertise. We included questions for the following types of experts: scientists; medical doctors; government officials; business leaders; religious leaders; journalists; lawyers; and scholars of history, philosophy, or English. Response options ranged from completely unwilling (0) to completely willing (6) (Vanderbilt University, undated). A summary score was computed as a mean response across these questions and ranged from 0 to 6.

One goal of this assessment was to allow a broader scope for facts and evidence than just scientific evidence. In particular, religious leaders, journalists, lawyers, and scholars in the humanities all purport to generate justified and true statements that specifically *do not* rely on scientific methods. In U.S. society, these experts (perhaps excluding the scientists) generally have a role in the interpretation of nonscientific facts and evidence. As a result, they could participate in processes related to Truth Decay; that is, the decline in the use of facts and evidence.[4] We note that these questions,

---

[4] Particular objection might be voiced to our inclusion of religious leaders in this list if *religion* is defined as encouraging people to endorse beliefs specifically because they do not have facts or evidence behind them, or even in the face of facts or evidence to the contrary. Faith in a higher being is not verifiable by scientific facts, but most religions have not conceived of themselves as endorsing faith against evidence; rather, they have seen themselves as possessing nonscientific forms of evidence—for example, miracles—that support their faith positions. Furthermore, religious leaders play an important role in the dissemination of information that much of our society has regarded as a kind of truth. Thus, a decline in trust of religious leaders may be correlated with other similar components of Truth Decay.

which capture a willingness to accept expert recommendations,[5] might raise concerns among more-scientific readers if these readers see trust in expertise itself as anathema to the use of facts and evidence. Ideally, all individuals would have the time, substantive knowledge, and experience to seek out the best data and full information on all topics to inform their decisions. In such a world, acceptance of expertise would not be needed because anyone could gain the requisite knowledge and information on any topic. But such an ideal becomes unattainable as the amounts and specificity of data and evidence become more extensive—and as many fields in the hard and social sciences, arts, applied technology, languages, and so on become more specialized. In this world, acceptance of (and even deference to) expertise and the ability to identify relevant experts becomes necessary and valuable. Those who continue to deny or reject the value of expertise, in effect, suggest that they themselves have the depth of knowledge necessary to make judgments on all matters. None of us can, in fact, be an expert on everything; so, taken to its extreme, broad rejection of expertise may suggest an inability or unwillingness to fully grapple with the enormity of facts and information available when forming judgments and opinions. It is for this reason that we believe these acceptance-of-experts questions are valuable.

Acceptance of expertise might even play a role in the process of scientific knowledge formation when viewed through the lens of peer review. Certainly, willingness to accept expert recommendations plays no formal role in the scientific method, which relies on the ability of independent observers to verify or falsify each other's claims through reference to repeatably observable empirical data (Butterfield, 1957). But, the evolution and generation of scientific knowledge routinely relies on peer review as a central and indispensable process. Peer review relies on the judgments of experts. Peer reviews act as an expert evaluation to prevent a scientific and lay audience from being misinformed or deceived by poor research, most particularly in the case that the lay audience is judged as being unable to evaluate the evidence as well as the experts can. Thus, although deference to experts plays no formal role in sci-

---

[5] See the section titled "Rejection of False Conspiracy Theories" in Appendix A.

entific justifications that are derived through the scientific method, it is paradoxically central to the modern production of scientific knowledge.[6]

We further note that we asked about classes of experts (for example, doctors, scientists, and journalists) and asked respondents whether they would accept the recommendation of those experts within their domain of expertise (however the respondents themselves delimited that). We think the questions, asked in this way, pertain to the traditional role of expertise in democratic societies, such as that of the United States. Modern democracies are sustained by institutions that are themselves sustained by classes of experts trained in particular roles. Autocracies, in contrast, are frequently centered on a cult of personality that surrounds a particular person (the autocrat). Acceptance of recommendations by one particular authority might be a kind of respect for experts, but it is not the kind of acceptance of expertise that has guided U.S. democracy. The latter has relied on *classes of experts*, which is what we asked about.

Shifting the Balance of Philosophical Positivism Versus Skepticism

Overarching philosophical perspectives about the objectivity of truth itself might underlie or derive from the Truth Decay trends articulated in Kavanagh and Rich (2018). We assessed individuals on their inclinations to positivism (that is, that there is some external standard of truth) in an exploratory way with two items. One asked about agreement with the statement that the scientific method was the best way to achieve knowledge when applicable,

---

[6] In the Foreword to a series on medieval thinkers, Brian Davies aptly summarized modernity's conflicted epistemology of trust in experts:

> It is certainly true that many medieval thinkers believed in authority (especially religious authority) as a serious court of appeal; and it is true that most people today would say that they cannot do this. Yet authority is as much an ingredient in our thinking as it was for medieval thinkers. For most of what we take ourselves to know is derived from the trust we have reposed in our various teachers, colleagues, friends, and general contacts. When it comes to reliance on authority, the main difference between us and medieval thinkers lies in the fact that their reliance on authority (insofar as they had it) was often more focused and explicitly acknowledged than is ours (Davies, 2000, p. x).

and the other asked about agreement with the statement that there are objective standards for right and wrong. This question—appropriately, we think—did not ask respondents to properly explain the scientific method. Instead, we asked whether it was the best way to achieve knowledge when applicable under whatever the respondent's understanding of the scientific method was and their understanding of its range of applicability. Response options ranged from strongly disagree (0) to strongly agree (5). An "unsure" option was also provided, to distinguish it from neither agree nor disagree. A summary score was computed as the average of all available responses and ranged from 0 to 5.[7] We were particularly interested in how self-reported attitudes toward the objectivity of truth correspond to the other identified aspects of Truth Decay.

Potential for Researcher Bias to Influence Item Development

Before diving into the results, we wish to note at the outset that it would be possible in this study, as in any study, for biases from the researcher, the institutions of science, or both to influence the results and thereby the conclusions. The primary concern for bias would be the selection or exclusion of items in the survey because these generate all the data. Biases within the data sampled are less of a concern because we performed a set of three analytic approaches with varying levels of assumptions and robusticity to bias. However, such analyses cannot correct for items that were never included in the study.

Correcting Biases of the Research Team

One form of bias would be from the researchers themselves. Researchers, being human, might carry personal experiences into their research in a manner that influences survey item selection. Clark and Tetlock (2022) advocated "adversarial collaboration" as a means to correct this form of bias, which meant composing research teams of researchers from varied and even conflicting

---

[7] "Unsure" responses for this section were handled in the same way as they were for the endorsement of false conspiracy theories scale, described earlier in this chapter and detailed in Chapter Five.

ideological viewpoints. We adopted this approach in this study. The coauthor team is disciplinarily diverse: The lead author, Matthews, is an anthropologist and accordingly skeptical of claims that such cultural phenomena as Truth Decay are even explainable in terms of individual-level variation. Coauthors Parker and Carman—a decision scientist and economist, respectively—are skeptical of most claims involving processes that do not reduce to individual-level variation. The coauthors also hold a variety of political and religious beliefs.[8] This led to the inclusion of items that would otherwise have been omitted. Matthews proposed asking about accepting recommendations by religious leaders, the verifiable fact questions about drone strikes and U.S. demographic changes, and the two questions about philosophical positivism versus skepticism. His intuition was that religious people and other conservatives might answer these more accurately than would liberals or nonreligious respondents, or that these questions might be particularly informative about religious and conservative panelists in the sample. Through a process of debate and discussion, the team agreed to include these items.

However, adversarial collaboration will primarily correct for biases in survey items that are developed by the team in question. In this study, our team developed only the verifiable fact and philosophical positivism questions. The other items were pulled, largely unaltered, from existing publications. Although these other items might have biases present in them, this bias (with respect to our study) would be a form of *institutional bias*, which occurs when the institutions of social systems are biased and the individuals who then inherit these institutional social structures thereby re-create biased outcomes even in the absence of biased cognitive processes in their own minds. For example, we used previously published survey items for our assessments of endorsement of scientific consensus, rejection of false conspiracy theories, and ability to distinguish fact from opinion; and most of the questions on willingness to accept expert recommendations were also from previously published material. It is possible that those published items on these topics are biased against Republicans, Black Americans, or other groups. For example, there might exist some other set of scientific topics that

---

[8]   Matthews is a religious Catholic, a weekly religious service attender, and has voted for the Republican governor of his state in multiple elections. He greatly enjoys robust debates with coauthor Parker, who is a nonreligious person from a Protestant background.

have not been asked about and on which White, educated Democrats consistently underperform. Our study would then re-create this form of bias as an institutional bias of the scientific process itself, in which researchers like ourselves routinely rely on previously published results to guide research. If those published results are biased, then no amount of adversarial collaboration would correct the institutionalized biased practices.

Correcting Institutional Biases

Our development and inclusion of new items is one attempt to avoid institutional bias in our measurement of the resistance/susceptibility to Truth Decay outcome. However, we had to do this while keeping within the scientific tradition that builds incrementally from prior research. Thus, we also relied on previously published item sets for several of the theorized scales of Truth Decay. We hope we have balanced these competing goals of avoiding institutionalized bias while participating in the institutions of science.

Another opportunity we saw to correct potential institutional biases was to collect a broader set of demographic information than is standard for nationally representative survey samples. Although race, income, and educational level are collected routinely, political and religious affiliation are not. Usually, these variables are excluded from studies unless they are research hypotheses of specific interest, whereas race typically is included as a covariate regardless of whether it is germane to the research hypotheses.

This institutionalized practice by social scientists might constitute a form of institutionalized racism, however, in that it creates greater opportunity to find differences between Black and White populations than to find differences within White populations or within Black populations. White Americans are the numerically much larger group in the United States, so we might expect this population to exhibit greater variance across subcultural categories (such as political affiliation) than variances exhibited within the Black American population or other minority groups, if only because larger group size can present more opportunity for cultural variation, assuming constant per capita rates of cultural innovation (see quantitative models in Boyd and Richerson, 1985). Several scholars have further highlighted how the focus on measuring contrasts between White Americans as a group and minority groups (such as Black Americans) obscures substantial variation within those minority groups and reinforces the race concept as a defining feature of U.S. society by omitting measurement of potentially more meaningful drivers of variation (Celious and Oyserman 2001; Drouhot and Garip, 2021).

In our study, we attempted to break out of a racializing dialectic of research to offer equal opportunity for both race and subcultural variation among White and Black populations (indexed by politics and religion) to predict data outcomes. We did this not to downplay racial disparities but rather to create an opportunity to find meaningful predictors of variation that are underappreciated because they do not fit within the racialized narrative that is used by most social scientists on both the political left and right. The persistence of not addressing variation within racial groups has the potential to recapitulate, as a bias of the research process itself, findings that Black Americans are different from White Americans even when such differences might not appear in comparisons with large and meaningful White cultural subgroups or when White Americans might have greater difference among themselves than they do with the Black population as a whole.

CHAPTER THREE

Identifying Reasoning Processes and Cognitive Biases Relevant to Resistance/Susceptibility to Truth Decay

To assess how reasoning processes and cognitive biases might be related to resistance/susceptibility to Truth Decay, we had to determine a set of processes and biases that each were measurable through a brief set of survey items. Over at least the past 50 years, the study of human decisionmaking has identified a wide variety of cognitive processes that influence decisions and biases (Gilovich, Griffin, and Kahneman, 2002; Kahneman, 2011). Truth Decay, at its root, is a set of phenomena regarding how people process and make judgments about information. Here, we sought to canvass the broad set of identified biases (and the underlying processes implicated by those biases) for those most likely to play a role in promoting (or mitigating) Truth Decay. Our goal was to cast a wide net while prioritizing those biases that both lent themselves to simple survey administration and presented the greatest expected opportunity for impact, recognizing that in one project we could only address a fraction of the potential space of cognitive biases. Additional detail and discussion of our methods is contained in Appendix C.

Selecting Cognitive (and Social) Biases for Inclusion

Our first step was to determine the set of biases that would be included in our analysis and about which we would ask in our survey. Drawing on a literature review, online searches, and expert judgment, we compiled a list of potential cognitive biases and cognitive processes. We then leveraged the diverse disciplinary makeup of our team (anthropology, economics, psychology, political science) and had each researcher independently rate 186 proposed biases or processes for relevance on a four-point scale. Each researcher then sorted the 48 items judged to be most relevant into conceptually related piles (Bernard, 1994). We did not specify in advance what these piles should be, and researchers grouped their piles using their own organizing structure. The researchers then discussed their piles to

- identify where consensus existed on piles and seek consensus where it did not already exist
- come to consensus on which biases belonged in which pile
- identify piles, and biases within piles, that provided the best opportunities for measurement in a survey.

For the last item, we assessed these opportunities according to whether existing published literature supported the idea that the bias or process could be assessed through well-understood and validated tasks.

Using this approach, we chose to focus on the following biases for this project:

1. **Availability bias** (Tversky and Kahneman, 1974). Events that are easier to recall are also judged as more likely (the availability heuristic), which can cause likelihood judgments to be biased toward more-salient or more-memorable events. For Truth Decay, distortion of risk perceptions should lead to disagreement regarding objective risk information.

2. **Unjustified confidence** (Parker and Stone, 2014). An updated conceptualization of the older idea of overconfidence, this is confidence in knowledge (or perceived knowledge) that is unrelated to actual knowledge. A lack of understanding of the extent of one's own knowledge has the potential to limit information-seeking and to increase rejection of expert judgment.

3. **Ingroup bias** (Inglehart and Baker, 2000; Newheiser et al., 2015; Wilkins-Laflamme, 2018). This refers to a set of interrelated tenden-

cies to feel more warmly toward one's cultural ingroup and to prefer them as partners during social interactions. Biases in favor of one's own cultural group (for example, as defined by language, religion, or nationality) might cognitively motivate skewed interpretations of facts in evidence.

Each of these biases is hypothesized to be associated with greater susceptibility to Truth Decay and to be feasible to measure in a brief online survey.

We did explore single items for three additional biases (susceptibility to the law of small numbers and two types of framing effect) but do not discuss those further here. (These and all other survey items are described in Appendix A.) It should also be noted that these do not represent the only biases deemed relevant to resistance/susceptibility to Truth Decay—merely those that best satisfied all our criteria.

In particular, there were other prominent biases, such as confirmation bias (Klayman and Ha, 1987) and myside bias (Stanovich, West, and Toplak, 2013), that were clearly relevant to resistance/susceptibility to Truth Decay but were not desirable in some other way—for example, they could not be easily assessed in a short online survey. Stanovich, West, and Toplak (2013) summarized that *myside bias* "occurs when people evaluate evidence, generate evidence, and test hypotheses in a manner biased toward their own prior opinions and attitudes." That report proceeds to make clear that myside bias is a cognitive process that purports to explain why individuals have poor justifications for their beliefs; it is because their myside bias induces them to interpret evidence to be consistent with their already held behaviors or opinions. *Confirmation bias* is similar and can be summarized as an individual's tendency to seek out evidence that confirms existing opinions while ignoring or discounting contradictory information.

Although both confirmation bias and myside bias might explain some aspects of the Truth Decay phenomenon, they are not synonymous with it because Truth Decay is a phenomenon to be explained (the *explanandum*), not an explanation itself. Truth Decay is a historically and culturally specific manifestation of a collective decline in the use of facts and evidence and an attendant decrease in truthful views. It is driven not only by biases and the way that humans process information but also by changes in information technology, the patterns of information production and consumption that result, and the political and social context in which information-sharing and knowledge production occur. Biases might not play a specific role in these other types of drivers of Truth Decay. Individuals might adopt untruthful beliefs for reasons not explained and then contort facts and evidence through the process of myside bias to match their beliefs. But biases do not tell the whole story. For example, biases do not explain the role played by information technology in spreading false information, nor do they capture the very intentional adoption of false narratives to serve an explicit political or economic aim with no effort to use facts and evidence as justification.

We also identified three reasoning processes that could be associated with susceptibility to Truth Decay. A reasoning process is a set of cognitive operations that work together according to a particular logic or domain of thought and that are more extensive in scope than a more singular bias, which could be inserted within many cognitive pathways. Reasoning processes that were implicated in resistance/susceptibility to Truth Decay included

- **numeracy**, or skill with numbers, which has been shown to be a pervasive predictor of a wide variety of biases and decisionmaking behaviors (Peters, 2020; Weller et al., 2013)
- **scientific reasoning**, which extends the older concept of science literacy and has recently been identified as a potential driver of behaviors rejecting scientific consensus (for example, rejecting climate change and vaccine safety) (Drummond and Fischhoff, 2017; Drummond and Fischhoff, 2019)
- **magical reasoning**, which includes a variety of superstitious beliefs (Rosengren and French, 2013) and at least conceptually represents a counterpoint to logical and scientific reasoning.

Drawing on the definitions of each of these processes, we hypothesized that greater numeracy and scientific reasoning would be associated with greater resistance to Truth Decay, whereas greater magical reasoning would be associated with greater susceptibility to Truth Decay.

Of the six reasoning processes and biases on which we focused, four items—numeracy, scientific reasoning, availability bias, and unjustified confidence—were performance tasks asking the respondent to answer questions that presented a challenge as accurately as possible. The other two items—magical reasoning and ingroup bias—should be regarded as self-reported items because these were agree-or-disagree response items that, in theory and for a variety of reasons, respondents could have answered in ways that did not reflect their actual views.

Identifying and Developing Reasoning and Bias Indicators

Our survey included six measures of cognitive biases and reasoning. The full text of the survey is available in Appendix A. Wherever possible, we capitalized on existing validated measures, which were more readily available for the reasoning constructs. When existing validated measures were not available, we developed new measures, taking lessons from existing approaches for assessing individual differences in cognitive biases (Bruine de Bruin, Parker, and Fischhoff, 2007; Stanovich, West, and Toplak, 2016). The measures are summarized in Table 3.1. The first three rows of the table reflect measures of reasoning; the last three reflect measures of cognitive bias.

We used a validated numeracy scale proposed by Weller et al. (2013), which builds off prior measures (for example, Lipkus, Samsa, and Rimer, 2001; Schwartz et al., 1997) but performs better across different ages and education levels. This eight-item measure assesses the ability of an individual to reason with numbers, and it emphasizes probabilistic reasoning. Each

TABLE 3.1

Measures of Reasoning and Cognitive Bias

Reasoning or Bias Construct	Source	Number of Items
Numeracy	Weller et al., 2013	8
Scientific reasoning	Drummond and Fischhoff, 2017	4
Magical reasoning	Eckblad and Chapman, 1983; Kingdon, Egan, and Rees, 2012	7
Availability bias	Developed for this report	6
Unjustified confidence	Parker and Stone, 2014	1
Ingroup bias	Inglehart and Baker, 2000; Inglehart and Welzel, 2010	10

item is scored as correct or incorrect, with nonresponses scored as incorrect, and the overall score is the number of items scored as correct, from 0 to 8.

The validated 11-item Scientific Reasoning Scale (Drummond and Fischhoff, 2017) assesses the ability to evaluate scientific evidence in terms of the factors that determine its quality. We used four items from this scale, selected in consultation with the scale's first author. Past research has shown that higher scores correlate positively with endorsement of scientific consensus on such issues as the safety of vaccines and genetically modified food, human evolution, and the Big Bang (Drummond and Fischhoff, 2017). As with numeracy, each item is scored as correct or incorrect, with nonresponses scored as incorrect, and the overall score is the number of items scored as correct, from 0 to 4.

For magical reasoning (a self-reported measure), we adapted prior scales to create a new seven-item scale focused on the core features of magical reasoning that was informed by previous scales that used many more items (Eckblad and Chapman, 1983 [30 items]; Kingdon, Egan, and Rees, 2012 [27 items]). We adopted Rosengren and French's (2013) cross-cultural view of core aspects of magical reasoning to reduce and simplify the items from these longer instruments. We selected from among those items by consulting ethnographic work on common cross-cultural features of magic. Thus, we included items that focused on two cross-culturally pervasive features of magic: magic by similarity and magic by contagion (Rosengren and French, 2013). The concept of *magic by similarity* involves the notion that similar objects share some magical essence (for example, photos of deceased people used in séances); the concept of *magic by contagion* attributes physical connectivity to moral virtue or repugnance (for example, imagine wearing Adolf Hitler's sweater).

We further excluded from our instrument supernatural beliefs that were expressly derived from traditional Judeo-Christian religious systems, such as belief in angels or the power of prayer. We did this for several reasons. First, we asked individuals their self-reported religious affiliation and frequency of attendance at religious services each as separate items. These questions likely are correlated with Judeo-Christian beliefs and thus capture this variation. Second, Kingdon, Egan, and Rees (2012) showed that traditional religious beliefs (for example, angels and prayer), appeared to be a separate and uncorrelated element of variation compared with beliefs in supernatural contagion and similarity. Third, although both magic and religion involve beliefs in the supernatural, sociologists of religion have theorized that they serve different purposes to the believer. Magic practitioners and consumers seek to control unseen forces by compelling them with the aim of affecting observable reality by preventing bad luck, bringing good luck, inducing romantic love, and so on. Practitioners and consumers of religion seek to supplicate unseen agents (gods) who can and do refuse supplications that mostly are oriented toward affecting a nonobservable reality, such as salvation in a future kingdom or afterlife (Stark, 2001). Thus, we selected items from among the published instruments that focused on magical contagion or similarity and were not aspects of traditional Judeo-Christian beliefs. It should be noted that the published instruments we consulted also did not include magical beliefs traditional to religions outside Judaism or Christianity.

To address availability bias, we developed six items that asked respondents which of two events occurred more frequently. For example, one question asked, "In a typical year, are more people in the U.S. attacked by sharks or killed by lightning?" (More people are killed by lightning.) In each case, questions were designed such that respondents would be more likely to encounter information regarding the less frequent event (for example, as presented in the media), thus likely making it more available in memory (Tversky and Kahneman, 1974).[1] Evidence suggests that events that are more widely reported (for example, homicides rather than suicides) are judged to be more likely to occur (Combs and Slovic, 1979). Each item was scored as correct or incorrect, and a total score was computed as the percentage of correct responses out of all items responded to. A similar task, the risk knowledge subtest of the Comprehensive Assessment of Rational Thinking (CART) (Stanovich, West, and Toplak, 2016) also uses questions like this, but asks many more of them. Because of our desire to fully publish our scale, we were reluctant to use the CART items verbatim. (CART is a standardized instrument, and full CART scales are not publicly published to prevent the public from learning correct responses.)

---

[1] Although most of the reference events would be quite memorable if experienced personally, the events that we selected for all questions but one (question 4) are also relatively rare.

Confidence in knowledge was assessed using an item referencing our eight-item numeracy scale combined with our one item on the law of small numbers, asking respondents "Considering the nine questions involving numbers that you just answered, how many do you think you got correct?"[2] Proposed relatively recently, the concept of *unjustified confidence* is an alternative to the concept of *overconfidence* and is particularly useful as a predictor variable (Parker and Stone, 2014). Unjustified confidence is operationalized in regression models as the effect of confidence on a dependent variable (in this case, Truth Decay) after controlling for actual knowledge (here, numeracy plus the law of small numbers) (Parker and Stone, 2014). As noted, we measured the law of small numbers through a single item validated by Tversky and Kahneman (1974).

Ingroup bias (a self-reported measure) was assessed using the standardized ten-item scale from the World Values Survey (Inglehart and Baker, 2000; Inglehart and Welzel, 2010). Respondents were prompted to indicate groups that they would not like to have as neighbors (for example, drug addicts, people of a different race). We used a score based on principal component analysis (PCA), extracting the first principal component (PC) score.

---

[2] A second question, not used here, asked, "Considering the nine questions involving numbers that you just answered, what percent of ALP panelists do you think you scored better than?"

CHAPTER FOUR

Survey Administration and Analytic Approach

This chapter describes the methods used in our research, including the sample; covariates used in regression analysis; statistical weights; treatment of missing variables; and the analytic approach. Additional detail and discussion of our methods is contained in Appendix C.

RAND American Life Panel and Selected Sample

The RAND ALP consists of approximately 4,000 adults from across the United States. The ALP is a nationally representative panel that the RAND Corporation has used since 2006 to track individual attitudes toward a variety of social, economic, political, and other issues. Panel members are recruited to the ALP using probability-based sampling methods (such as address-based sampling and random-digit phone dialing). Panel members agree to respond to regular online surveys, typically two to three per month. To ensure the representativeness of the panel, individuals who did not previously have access to the internet were provided with a netbook computer and internet access. A core set of demographic variables are regularly collected from all ALP panelists; the most recent of these data are automatically merged with data from each survey. This increases the efficiency for new surveys, which do not need to collect these data. [1] A recent Pew Research Center report (Kennedy et al., 2020) demonstrates that probability-based panels, to which respondents are

---

[1] Additional information about the ALP is available at the ALP homepage (RAND Corporation, undated).

invited rather than opt in, show significantly lower rates of bogus responding than do convenience panels and other sample sources, such as job-sourcing services (for example, MTurk), where bogus responding is defined as providing non sequitur responses to open-ended questions or constant responses (that is, always box "a" or "b," etc.) to closed-ended questions.

For this study, we invited 1,626 ALP panelists. Of these, 1,333 completed the survey (81.9 percent completion rate). Respondents for this survey were selected from a group that had previously participated in surveys conducted during the 2016 presidential election and other past surveys on vaccination, numeracy, or trust in institutions. Our survey was fielded from February 26 through March 13, 2019.

Covariates

We considered a variety of socioeconomic and demographic variables along with religiosity, political affiliation, and voting behavior. These include age, gender, education, race or ethnicity,[2] whether the respondent was born in the United States, and household income.

Weighting and Treatment of Missing Data

Because all random samples differ from the overall population they are selected to represent, the ALP generates sampling weights, which can be applied to make the data as representative as possible. The ALP benchmarks the weights against the Current Population Survey, using a raking procedure involving gender, age, race or ethnicity, education, number of household members, and household income. Additional details are available in Pollard and Baird (2017).

Individual biases, reasoning measures, and indicators of resistance/ susceptibility to Truth Decay each were, by and large, assessed through mul-

---

[2] Throughout this analysis we treated Hispanic as a category exclusive of other racial groups. Individuals who identified as Hispanic were counted as this and not within any other racial groups with which they identified.

tiple survey questions to ensure that the results were robust to idiosyncrasies of interpretation of any single item. When respondents did not respond to items, we dropped those items from the analysis, treated nonresponses as incorrect, or dropped the items from individual scales. Additional information is available in Appendix C.

Analytic Approach

In Chapter Five, we describe our results. We first describe the sample (both before and after applying weights), using simple means, standard deviations, and percentages. Then, because many of the measures presented here are newly constructed, we provide summary statistics.

We next examine bivariate correlations among our variables of interest, both within and between variable sets.

Finally, to test our main hypothesis that resistance to Truth Decay is associated with less rigorous reasoning and greater cognitive bias, we conduct three sets of regression analyses. The first predicts each of our proposed measures of resistance/susceptibility to Truth Decay using our measures of reasoning and bias, both without and with controlling for the covariates already described.

The second regression analysis accounts for the possibility that our a priori grouping of survey items into scales of Truth Decay (for example, endorsement of verifiable facts, rejection of false conspiracy theories) does not reflect how Americans think about these issues. It is possible that we, as researchers, come to the table with our own misconceptions about how aspects of resistance/susceptibility to Truth Decay are organized. To analyze the data in a manner agnostic to our own grouping of survey items, we subjected the entire pool of individual Truth Decay items to PCA and extracted component scores for each individual item on each of the major components identified. Then, similar to the six a priori scales of resistance/susceptibility to Truth Decay, these component scores were treated with bivariate correlations and as outcome variables in regression models with reasoning, biases, and both with and without our demographic covariates as predictors.

The third set of regression analysis adopts an even more relativist stance than the second. In the second approach, we relaxed our own assumptions about how Truth Decay items fit into categories; in the third approach, we relaxed our assumptions about which answers to each Truth Decay item are "truth" versus "decay." Both the first and second sets of regression analysis orient the individual items from one end (which external scholarly standards generally indicate as resistance to Truth Decay) and the other end (thought of as susceptibility to Truth Decay). In this third approach, we instead considered whether individuals deviated from the "consensus truth" about these items, defined as multivariate agreement on the items across all respondents. This culturally relative notion is based on the conception that truth is a body of agreed beliefs that are shared by a society (Romney, Batchelder, and Weller, 1987; Romney, Weller, and Batchelder, 1986; Weller, 2007; Matthews, Brown, and Kennedy, 2018). Anthropologists working in cross-cultural settings developed Cultural Consensus Analysis (CCA) as a robust method for measuring each individual's relative agreement with the central tendency across all individuals and across all survey items. CCA uses inferred components, as does PCA, but in CCA, the loading of each individual respondent on the first component of the CCA reflects the level of agreement that an individual has with the central tendency of responses from all individuals and across all survey items (see Appendix C). Using this measured level of agreement as an outcome variable in regressions reflects how close (or distant) an individual's beliefs are from the average or most prototypical beliefs within the culture.

Because CCA is a less familiar technique to researchers outside anthropology, we provide the following example that provides an intuition for how the mathematics of CCA operates. It is based on recent applications of CCA to the study of eyewitness reports as a kind of microcultural tradition in which independent witnesses have differential knowledge of the crime. Video experiments have shown that CCA more accurately reconstructs witnessed events than does taking a simple majority interpretation from each survey item. This is because CCA privileges the majority interpretation of the multivariate agreement across all items, not each item individually (Waubert de Puiseau et al., 2012).

Consider a hypothetical crime in which a store is robbed and the robbers escape in a vehicle. Witnesses provide accounts with factual information, summarized in Table 4.1.

TABLE 4.1

Illustrative Example of Data Coded from Multiple Eyewitness Reports of a Hypothetical Robbery and Escape by Car

Individual	Shop Window Broken	Shop Door Broken	Suspect's Race	Car Color	Car Type
1	Yes	Yes	Black	Black	Van
2	No	Yes	Black	Green	Truck
3	Yes	No	Black	Blue	Sedan
4	Yes	No	South Asian	Blue	Sedan
5	Yes	No	South Asian	Blue	Sedan

CCA places more weight on the responses from the witnesses that are inferred to be more reliable because they agree with each other across the multivariate item set. This form of analysis then weights those responses more highly when creating an aggregated outcome. In the hypothetical example, CCA would conclude the suspect's race was South Asian, even though a majority of witnesses thought it was Black. This is because witnesses 3, 4, and 5 show strong agreement about the other elements of the report, such as the type of car and whether the shop window or door were broken, and a majority of those witnesses said that the suspect's race was South Asian. CCA infers from the observed variance across multiple items that witnesses 1 and 2 are less informed about the witnessed event.

Taken together, these analyses balance a priori views with data-driven views of the relationships among the Truth Decay indicators and with these indicators' relationships to the cognitive variables and covariates.

CHAPTER FIVE

Results

Sample Characteristics

Table 5.1 provides sample descriptive statistics, both unweighted and weighted. By and large, the ALP sample (unweighted) is similar to the population (as reflected in the weighted results). The ALP sample generally is over age 50, has higher income, and is more educated than the general population.

Properties of the Reasoning and Cognitive Bias Measures

Table 5.2 provides a summary of the numeracy, scientific reasoning, and magical reasoning measures, in terms of their mean, standard deviation (SD), and range. **Respondents, on average, answered just over one-half of the numeracy and scientific reasoning items correctly.** In line with prior studies of magical reasoning, we applied a PCA technique to extract a weighted average of the original items that maximizes the amount of variance explained by a single score.[1] Additional detail is presented in Appendix B.

---

[1] PCA is an exploratory data analysis technique that uses the observed correlations among a set of variables to construct new synthetic variables (components) that reflect the total variance across all the original variables but in a new set of uncorrelated components. Because PCA maximizes the amount of total variation on the first components, it frequently is used as a technique to reduce the number of variables in an analysis while maximizing the shared information among them.

TABLE 5.1

Unweighted and Weighted Sample Descriptive Statistics

Characteristic	Mean (SE)	Mean (SE)
Age	58.4 (0.38)	49.6 (0.99)
Female	47%	48%
Education		
Less than high school	2%	6%
High school	10%	32%
Some college	34%	27%
College degree	54%	35%
Household annual income		
Less than $25,000	14%	18%
$25,000 to $49,999	22%	24%
$50,000 to $74,999	21%	21%
$75,000 to $99,999	12%	10%
$100,000 to $124,999	13%	12%
$125,000 or more	18%	15%
Race or ethnicity		
Hispanic	11%	24%
Black, non-Hispanic	6%	7%
White, non-Hispanic	78%	65%
Asian, non-Hispanic	2%	2%
Other, non-Hispanic	2%	2%
Born in United States	93%	91%

Table 5.1—Continued

Characteristic	Mean (SE)	Mean (SE)
Religious affiliation		
Mainstream Protestant	23%	17%
Catholic	21%	23%
Evangelical or Pentecostal	5%	5%
Nondenominational Christian	17%	21%
Other Christian groups	3%	4%
Jewish	3%	2%
Other religions	4%	2%
No religious affiliation	13%	16%
Atheist or agnostic	10%	10%
Political affiliation		
Independent	29%	32%
Democrat	36%	32%
Republican	24%	22%
Vote in 2016		
Clinton	46%	44%
Trump	37%	36%
Other candidate or did not vote	16%	21%

NOTE: SE = standard error. N = 1,323 individuals; all items are self-reported.

TABLE 5.2

Summary Statistics of Three Reasoning Measures

Scale	Mean	SD	Minimum, Maximum
Numeracy	4.2	1.8	0, 8
Scientific reasoning	2.5	1.2	0, 4
Magical reasoning	0	1.6	−4.9, 3.7

Table 5.3 provides a summary of each of the three bias measures (availability bias, unjustified confidence, and ingroup bias), in terms of their mean, SD, and range.

Among the six newly constructed items assessing availability bias, difficulties (the percentage correct) ranged from 10 percent ("In a typical year, do more people in the U.S. die from motor vehicle accidents or poisoning?") to 91 percent ("In a typical year, is a person in the U.S. more likely to be struck by lightning or to win the Powerball lottery?"). **On average, respondents correctly answered 43 percent of the items.**

Unjustified confidence is determined relative to an objective measure of performance (in this case, on the eight numeracy items plus one law of small numbers item in the survey). On those, respondents on average estimated that they got 6.4 of 9 items correct (SD = 2.0). On average, however, they really only got 4.8 items correct (SD = 1.8). In terms of percentages, **this corresponds to being 17.7 percent overconfident, on average (6.4/9 minus 4.8/9).** For regression analyses, such as those reported later in this chapter, unjustified confidence is operationalized as the relationship of confidence (perceived number correct) with the dependent variable, after controlling for actual performance.

In line with prior studies of ingroup bias, we also applied PCA to extract a weighted average that accounts for the maximal amount of variation in the original items.

Table 5.4 presents correlations among the reasoning and bias measures. **Higher numeracy scores were strongly associated with greater sci-**

TABLE 5.3

Summary Statistics of Three Cognitive Bias Measures

Scale	Mean	SD	Minimum, Maximum
Availability bias	0.43	0.21	0, 1
Unjustified confidence			
Perceived number correct	6.4	2.0	0, 9
Actual number correct	4.8	1.8	0, 9
Ingroup bias	0.77	0.25	0, 1

TABLE 5.4

Pairwise Correlations Among Six Reasoning and Cognitive Bias Measures

Measure	1. Numeracy	2. Scientific Reasoning	3. Magical Reasoning	4. Availability Bias	5. Unjustified Confidence
1. Numeracy					
2. Scientific reasoning	0.46				
3. Magical reasoning	−0.07	−0.10			
4. Availability bias	−0.30	−0.23	0.02		
5. Unjustified confidence	0.00	−0.06	0.03	0.01	
6. Ingroup bias	−0.10	−0.01	−0.07	0.07	−0.04

NOTE: As is common with pairwise correlation notation, the correlation of A-B is the same mathematically as the correlation of B-A, so one-half of the matrix is left blank.

entific reasoning, and higher scores on each were weakly associated with less magical reasoning. Numeracy and scientific reasoning correlate negatively with availability bias. This set of results is consistent with either an underlying ability toward more analytic and less biased reasoning or a set of separate but mutually supportive skills. Magical reasoning, on the other hand, had near-zero correlations with the cognitive bias scores. Of particular interest, ingroup bias did not show substantial correlations with numeracy, scientific reasoning, or magical reasoning. This might be because it has more of a social or motivational component than do the more cognitive biases.

Properties of the Truth Decay Measures

Table 5.5 presents a summary of each of the six a priori scales of resistance/susceptibility to Truth Decay. Additional detail is presented in Appendix B.

On average, respondents displayed a relatively high rate of susceptibility to Truth Decay, as measured by these scales. They endorsed the scientific consensus on about one-half (3.2) of the six items, and endorsed 2.1 of the five verifiable facts. On average, respondents gave a response of 3.7 (just to the side of disagreement) regarding false conspiracy theories. On average, respondents were able to correctly distinguish news items that relied primarily on fact versus opinion 4.2 out of 6 times. They also tended to be in the middle of the scale for accepting recommendations from experts (3.3). Finally, respondents on average responded moderately in favor of positivism over skepticism (3.6 out of 5). Taken together, these suggest that many people who exhibit a degree of skepticism regarding science and news as traditional sources of truth have difficulties distinguishing fact from opinion.

As presented in Table 5.6, the six measures all intercorrelate moderately and positively, as might be expected if either they all reflect an underlying resistance to Truth Decay or, alternatively, they mutually support each other (Stanovich and West, 2000). The strongest correlations were (1) endorsement of scientific consensus and rejection of false conspiracy theories and (2) endorsement of verifiable fact and rejection of false conspiracy theories.

TABLE 5.5

Summary Statistics of Six a Priori Scales of Resistance/Susceptibility to Truth Decay

Scale	Mean	SD	Minimum, Maximum
Endorsement of scientific consensus	3.2	1.7	0, 6
Endorsement of verifiable facts	2.1	1.2	0, 5
Rejection of false conspiracy theories	3.7	1.0	0, 5
Ability to distinguish fact from opinion	4.2	1.3	1, 6
Willingness to accept expert recommendations	3.3	0.8	0, 6
Philosophical positivism versus skepticism	3.6	1.0	0, 5

TABLE 5.6

Pairwise Correlations Among Six a Priori Scales of Resistance/Susceptibility to Truth Decay

Measure	1	2	3	4	5
1					
2	0.31				
3	0.45	0.32			
4	0.31	0.15	0.20		
5	0.30	0.20	0.36	0.18	
6	0.30	0.20	0.16	0.23	0.13

NOTE: Measure key:
1 = Endorsement of scientific consensus
2 = Endorsement of verifiable facts
3 = Rejection of false conspiracy theories
4 = Willingness to accept expert recommendation
5 = Ability to distinguish fact from opinion
6 = Philosophical positivism versus skepticism

Predicting Resistance/Susceptibility to Truth Decay with Reasoning and Bias Measures

Table 5.7 presents the zero-order (that is, unadjusted) correlations between each of our initial measures of resistance/susceptibility to Truth Decay (columns) and each of our reasoning and bias measures (rows). We found the following:

- **Greater numeracy and scientific reasoning, as well as lower magical reasoning (self-reported), were associated with greater resistance to Truth Decay** as measured across our Truth Decay resistance/susceptibility indicators.
- **Endorsement of verifiable facts (self-reported) and philosophical positivism (self-reported) were more closely correlated with numeracy and scientific reasoning** than magical reasoning, whereas accepting expert recommendations was more closely associated with magical reasoning.
- **Greater susceptibility to availability bias was associated with modestly greater susceptibility to Truth Decay** across all indicators except accepting expert recommendations.
- **Ingroup bias (self-reported) was negatively correlated with endorsing scientific consensus and philosophical positivism** but positively correlated with rejecting false conspiracies and being able to distinguish fact from opinion.

Of course, these correlations are simply descriptions of unadjusted relationships. Although illustrative, a more nuanced view is provided by linear regression analyses, which can estimate the associations of each bias with resistance/susceptibility to Truth Decay after controlling for associations with the other biases in Table 5.7. Table 5.8 reveals the results of this analysis.

The results from Table 5.8 suggest that numeracy and scientific reasoning correlate positively with resistance to most a priori scales of resistance/susceptibility to Truth Decay, even after controlling for other measured biases and reasoning processes. Conversely, magical reasoning (self-reported) is negatively associated with resistance to most categories of Truth Decay, as is availability bias. Ingroup bias (self-reported)

TABLE 5.7

Correlations Between Resistance to Truth Decay and Measures of Reasoning or Cognitive Bias

Measure	Endorsement of Scientific Consensus	Endorsement of Verifiable Facts	Rejection of False Conspiracy Theories	Ability to Distinguish Fact from Opinion	Willingness to Accept Expert Recommendations	Philosophical Positivism Versus Skepticism
Numeracy	0.36	0.31	0.33	0.32	0.08	0.19
Scientific reasoning	0.30	0.25	0.30	0.31	0.00	0.10
Magical reasoning	−0.20	−0.03	−0.17	−0.14	−0.16	−0.06
Availability bias	−0.20	−0.17	−0.23	−0.16	0.06	−0.14
Unjustified confidence	−0.00	0.08	0.01	−0.00	0.10	0.04
Ingroup bias	−0.31	−0.13	0.38	0.37	0.06	−0.41

TABLE 5.8

Multiple Linear Regression of a Priori Scales of Resistance to Truth Decay on Biases and Reasoning Processes

Predictor Variable (measure of reasoning or cognitive bias)	Regression Coefficients (unstandardized)					
	Endorsement of Scientific Consensus	Endorsement of Verifiable Facts	Rejection of False Conspiracy Theories	Ability to Distinguish Fact from Opinion	Willingness to Accept Expert Recommendations	Philosophical Positivism Versus Skepticism
Numeracy	0.17***	0.09***	0.11***	0.16***	0.03	0.06**
Scientific reasoning	0.22***	0.11***	0.11***	0.17***	-0.02	0.03
Magical reasoning	-0.23***	-0.10***	-0.15***	-0.06**	0.01	-0.02
Availability bias	-0.34	-0.25	-0.61***	-0.37*	0.28*	-0.31*
Unjustified confidence	-0.01	0.05**	0.02	0.02	0.05***	0.02
Ingroup bias	-0.39***	-0.10***	0.35***	0.42***	0.04*	-0.33***

Table 5.8—Continued

Predictor Variable (measure of reasoning or cognitive bias)	Regression Coefficients (unstandardized)					
	Endorsement of Scientific Consensus	Endorsement of Verifiable Facts	Rejection of False Conspiracy Theories	Ability to Distinguish Fact from Opinion	Willingness to Accept Expert Recommendations	Philosophical Positivism Versus Skepticism
Constant	2.10***	1.17***	3.09***	3.18***	2.77***	3.27***
Overall model performance						
R^2	0.28	0.14	0.37	0.3	0.03	0.2
Adjusted R^2	0.27	0.14	0.36	0.3	0.02	0.2
Residual SE (df = 1,291)	1.43	1.09	0.83	0.92	0.79	
F Statistic (df = 7; 1,291)	70.79***	31.17***	107.48***	78.81***	5.42***	46.03***

NOTE: * $p < 0.05$; ** $p < 0.01$; *** $p < 0.001$. Sample size = 1,299, df = degree of freedom.

shows the most complex relationship to the Truth Decay phenomenon; it is predictive of resistance to conspiracy theories and greater ability to distinguish fact from opinion but less so of endorsement of scientific consensus and verifiable facts (self-reported) and of philosophical positivism (self-reported).

These findings, however, highlight the need to consider other covariates of Truth Decay, such as demographic factors, that might themselves be correlated with the development of biases or reasoning processes. For example, scientific reasoning ability likely develops through formal education and through informal educational exposures in the home, and these are associated with numerous other unmeasured factors. We might wish to know whether scientific reasoning ability predicts resistance/susceptibility to Truth Decay after controlling for a direct effect of education and home environment. Similarly, ingroup bias (favoring one's own ethnocultural group) might be correlated with certain demographics in U.S. society; for example, White and wealthier individuals might be expected to have more ingroup bias. If such race and wealth variables are correlated with unmeasured processes that promote resistance to Truth Decay (such as access to better schools or more books in the home), then this would create a spurious association of ingroup bias with resistance to Truth Decay in a regression that does not account for demographic predictor variables. Put more generally, the specific associations of cognitive processes, such as ingroup bias, and resistance/susceptibility to Truth Decay might vary across societies and historical contexts if these associations are driven more by idiosyncrasies of culture history than by actual functional links between cognition and resistance/susceptibility to Truth Decay

Case Study of Acceptance of Expert Recommendations and Institutional Bias

Before delving into how the use of demographic covariates alters our multiple regression models, we wish to illustrate how our use of a broader set of demographics (political and religious affiliation) might enable better control for sociocultural variation and in a manner that avoids institutional biases of typical survey research.

Prior studies have shown that, compared with White Americans, Black Americans have a tendency toward less acceptance of expert recommendations and more endorsement of related ideas, such as conspiracy theories (Uscinski and Parent, 2014; Westergaard et al., 2014; Bogart et al., 2021; Matthews et al., 2022). This has been most evaluated, however, specifically in the context of acceptance of recommendations by medical experts. How subsets of White individuals, such as White Republicans versus White Democrats, differ in this feature has not been much evaluated in prior nationally representative survey samples. If questions that show Black Americans are less accepting of recommendations by a class of experts (such as medical doctors) are valid for identifying a racial difference, it stands to reason that they are valid for identifying a political difference within a single racial group (that is, among White individuals).

Plotting the summed willingness to accept expert recommendations score for Black respondents,[2] White Republican respondents, and White Democratic respondents reveals that the main difference in this variable is a different mean level between White Republican respondents and White Democratic respondents (Figure 5.1). The summed score for accepting expert recommendations for the group of Black respondents was in the middle of the distributions for the two White groups. This reveals the type of enhanced variation among the numerically larger White American population that can go unnoticed in studies that do not analyze subcultural variation among White individuals. Failure to measure variation among White subgroups can result in the finding of Black-White average differences, reifying the race concept as genetically or culturally instantiated difference, when the more meaningful variation is really among White subgroups. When considered by political party, White Democratic respondents were more accepting of expert recommendations than were Black respondents (although not significantly so, at a 0.05 significance level), while White Republicans were least accepting of expert recommendations among all three groups, at a statistically significant level (Figure 5.1). Thus, the most meaningful variation in these data is the pattern in which White Republican respondents differ from the other two groups, but this would

---

[2] Black respondents in our sample all identified as politically Democratic or independent; none were Republicans.

FIGURE 5.1

Summed Scores for Accepting Expert Recommendations by Race and Political Party Affiliation

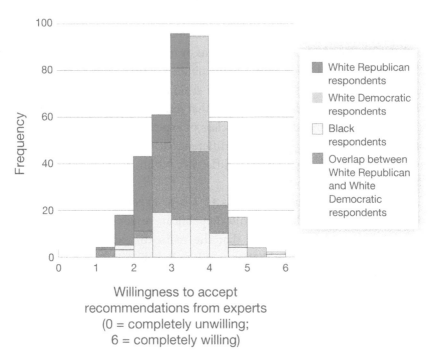

Willingness to accept recommendations from experts
(0 = completely unwilling;
6 = completely willing)

NOTES: Of 81 Black respondents in our sample, 61 were Democrats, 20 were independents, and none were Republicans.

have gone unnoticed if we had followed standard social science practices and included race among our "standard" demographic characteristics and excluded political party affiliation.

We can further investigate these patterns using the items about expert recommendations (Table 5.9). Examining the question about accepting expert recommendations from medical doctors individually, we see the most commonly measured pattern in the literature: Black respondents were less accepting of recommendations by the medical establishment than were White respondents (matching findings by, for example, Westergaard et al., 2014; Bogart et al., 2021; and Matthews et al., 2022). However, we also see that fewer White Republican respondents than White Democratic respondents said that they would accept recommendations from medical doctors.

TABLE 5.9

Mean Scores on the Question of Accepting Expert Recommendations

Expert Category	Black Respondents	White Republican Respondents	White Democratic Respondents
Scientists	4.04 [3.80–4.28]	3.97 [3.85–4.08]	**4.95 [4.84–5.05]**
Medical doctors	4.06 [3.82–4.30]	4.43 [4.32–4.54]	**4.75 [4.65–4.84]**
Government officials	2.62 [2.35–2.88]	2.20 [2.06–2.33]	2.85 [2.71–2.99]
Business leaders	**3.17 [2.89–3.45]**	**3.25 [3.12–3.38]**	2.74 [2.62–2.86]
Religious leaders	**3.40 [3.05–3.74]**	**3.47 [3.33–3.62]**	2.22 [2.04–2.39]
Journalists	3.01 [2.75–3.28]	1.72 [1.56–1.87]	**3.68 [3.55–3.80]**
Lawyers[a]	3.15 [2.79–3.50]	2.74 [2.57–2.91]	**3.27 [3.13–3.42]**
Scholars of history, philosophy, or English	3.91 [3.62–4.21]	3.41 [3.28–3.55]	**4.37 [4.25–4.49]**

NOTES: 95% confidence intervals are shown in brackets. Green shaded cells are not statistically different. High ends of the trust scales are bolded.

[a] Black respondents overlap with the two groups of White respondents, who do not overlap.

The same is true for accepting recommendations by scientists—but, in this case, Black respondents and White Republican respondents were equally accepting, while White Democratic respondents were more accepting of scientist recommendations.

Recommendations by government officials were least accepted by White Republican respondents; however, all three groups were more skeptical than accepting of recommendations by government officials.

Recommendations of business and religious leaders were least accepted by White Democratic respondents; Black respondents and White Republican respondents were both more accepting and were not significantly different from each other. For each of the categories of journalists, lawyers, and scholars of the humanities, White Democratic respondents were the most accepting of these experts' recommendations, Black respondents exhibited middle levels of acceptance, and White Republican respondents were the least accepting. In summary, across all these questions, we obtained results that cut against the typical racialized narrative that the most fundamental distinction in U.S. society falls along Black-White lines.

Unpacking the results about acceptance of expert recommendations items individually, as outlined above, underscores the point that those doing future research on Truth Decay, misinformation, and related concepts might be well advised to measure subcultural variation, especially in the White majority population. Only by measuring this variation is there the opportunity for the data to transcend standard racialized dialectics. The United States is not a postracial society, but in virtually every row of Table 5.9, race is not the most important variable for understanding variation in acceptance of recommendations by experts. Although the results show Black respondents had a unique pattern, they were the least accepting *only* of recommendations by medical doctors. For every other category of expert, Black respondents either statistically overlapped with one of the White groups or fell between them statistically.

Multiple Regression Results That Include Demographic Variables

We can make additional headway toward understanding the potential role of biases, after controlling for direct demographic effects, through a multiple regression that includes such demographic covariates as age, gender, and education. Table 5.10 presents linear regression analyses predicting each of our six indicators of resistance/susceptibility to Truth Decay with (1) demographic and social characteristics, (2) reasoning processes, and (3) cognitive biases.

As can be seen in Table 5.10, **the bias measures often remain significantly associated with a priori scales of resistance/susceptibility to Truth Decay even after controlling for demographic factors.** We find these results compelling in that we control for a wide set of demographic factors, which themselves are also often significant. Overall, the regression models account for between 15 percent (accept recommendations by experts) and 49 percent (rejection of false conspiracy theories) of the variance in the a priori scales of resistance/susceptibility to Truth Decay. We also observed the following regarding the bias measures:

- After controlling for demographic and social covariates, **greater numeracy and scientific reasoning skills were associated with greater resis-**

TABLE 5.10

Multiple Linear Regression Predicting a Priori Scales of Resistance/Susceptibility to Truth Decay

Predictor Variable	Regression Coefficients (unstandardized)					
	Endorsement of Scientific Consensus	Endorsement of Verifiable Facts	Rejection of False Conspiracy Theories	Ability to Distinguish Fact from Opinion	Willingness to Accept Expert Recommendations	Philosophical Positivism Versus Skepticism
Age	0.005	0.01***	0.01***	-0.01**	-0.003	0.001
Female	-0.06	-0.27***	-0.07	0.002	0.03	-0.11
Education						
Less than high school	-0.08	-0.11	-0.27	0.02	-0.13	-0.19
Some college	0.01	0.13	0.02	-0.002	-0.11	-0.1
College degree	0.31*	0.26*	0.15	0.17	-0.02	-0.06
Income midpoint (divided by 10,000)	0.02***	0.02**	0.02***	0.01*	0.01***	0.02**
Race						
Hispanic (n = 148)	-0.41**	-0.18	-0.40***	-0.27*	0.11	-0.16
Black, non-Hispanic (n = 81)	-0.82***	-0.13	-0.55***	-0.49***	-0.13	-0.2
Asian, non-Hispanic (n = 33)	-0.54*	-0.21	-0.35*	-0.24	-0.26	-0.44*
Other, non-Hispanic (n = 26)	-0.96***	0.04	-0.37*	-0.37	-0.38*	-0.14
Born in United States	-0.17	0.21	-0.19*	-0.01	-0.03	-0.16

Table 5.10—Continued

Predictor Variable	Regression Coefficients (unstandardized)					
	Endorsement of Scientific Consensus	Endorsement of Verifiable Facts	Rejection of False Conspiracy Theories	Ability to Distinguish Fact from Opinion	Willingness to Accept Expert Recommendations	Philosophical Positivism Versus Skepticism
Religion						
Mainstream Protestant	-0.17	0.16	0.01	-0.13	0.05	-0.02
Evangelical or Pentecostal	-0.56**	0.28	-0.19	-0.21	0.24*	0.04
Nondenominational Christian	-0.44***	0.23*	-0.13	-0.07	0.05	0.07
Other Christian groups	-0.05	0.29	0.06	-0.31	-0.04	0.05
Jewish	-0.13	-0.23	-0.07	0.09	-0.07	0.11
Other religions	-0.3	0.23	-0.17	0.03	0.02	0.17
No religious affiliation	-0.25	-0.02	-0.09	-0.01	-0.15	-0.07
Atheist or agnostic	0.19	0.14	0.20*	0.24	-0.09	0.1
Religious service attendance	-0.13***	-0.04	-0.08***	0.01	0.002	0.03
Political affiliation						
Democrat	0.04	0.12	0.11	-0.06	0.22***	0.18*
Republican	-0.06	0.02	0.03	-0.08	0.04	-0.04
Clinton voter 2016	0.61***	0.17	0.22**	0.38***	0.29***	0.19*
Trump voter 2016	-0.67***	-0.03	-0.14*	0.08	-0.1	-0.17*

Table 5.10—Continued

Predictor Variable	Regression Coefficients (unstandardized)					
	Endorsement of Scientific Consensus	Endorsement of Verifiable Facts	Rejection of False Conspiracy Theories	Ability to Distinguish Fact from Opinion	Willingness to Accept Expert Recommendations	Philosophical Positivism Versus Skepticism
Measures of reasoning or cognitive bias						
Numeracy	0.10***	0.06*	0.05**	0.11***	0.02	0.03
Scientific reasoning	0.13***	0.09**	0.08***	0.12***	-0.04	0.003
Magical reasoning	-0.13***	-0.08***	-0.10***	-0.03	0.01	0.004
Availability bias	-0.25	0.005	-0.39***	-0.26	0.29**	-0.25
Unjustified confidence	0.01	0.02	0.02	0.03	0.05***	0.01
Ingroup bias	-0.41***	-0.10***	0.36***	0.42***	0.0003	-0.36***
Constant	2.53***	0.24	3.01***	3.51***	2.77***	3.37***
Overall model performance						
R^2	0.49	0.22	0.5	0.35	0.15	0.26
Adjusted R^2	0.48	0.2	0.49	0.34	0.13	0.25
Residual SE (df = 1,259)	1.21	1.05	0.74	1.03	0.75	0.89

NOTES: Base levels: male, high school, non-Hispanic White, born outside the United States, Catholic, independent voting affiliation, voted for other candidate in 2016. Responses of "unsure" have been recoded as the mean of an individual's responses to related questions. * $p < 0.05$; ** $p < 0.01$; *** $p < 0.001$. Sample size = 1,291.

tance to Truth Decay on all measures except accepting recommendations by experts and philosophical positivism (self-reported).

- Magical reasoning (self-reported) was the opposite, showing negative
associations with endorsement of scientific consensus and verifiable
facts and with rejection of false conspiracy theories.

- Greater availability bias was associated with greater susceptibility to
false conspiracy theories and simultaneously greater acceptance of
expert recommendations. The latter relationship only appeared after
controlling for the other predictors (that is, it was not apparent in the
pairwise correlation in Table 5.7).

- **Among the cognitive biases, ingroup bias (self-reported) was far and
away the strongest predictor, but as in the regression without demographic controls, it associates with resistance/susceptibility to Truth
Decay in differing directions.** Those displaying greater ingroup bias
were significantly less likely to endorse scientific consensus and verifiable facts, but were less susceptible to false conspiracy theories and
more able to distinguish fact from opinion. They were also significantly less likely to endorse philosophical positivism (or alternatively,
more likely to be philosophical skeptics).

Regarding the associations of resistance to Truth Decay with demographics, we found the following:

- **Adults over 50 were more likely to endorse verifiable facts and reject
false conspiracy theories.**
- Men were more likely to endorse verifiable facts.
- **Those with higher household incomes (self-reported) demonstrated
greater resistance to Truth Decay across all scales.**
- **Relative to non-Hispanic White respondents (self-reported), racial
and ethnic minorities showed greater susceptibility to Truth Decay,**
as indicated by a lack of endorsement of scientific consensus; acceptance of false conspiracy theories; and, for Black respondents, greater
difficulty distinguishing fact from opinion.
- There were no strong patterns across religious affiliations (self-reported)
except that evangelical, Pentecostal, and nondenominational Christians
exhibited less endorsement of scientific consensus. Also, those reporting

greater religious attendance tended to exhibit less endorsement of scientific consensus and less rejection of false conspiracy theories.

- Finally, **those who reported voting for Clinton in the 2016 election showed greater endorsement of scientific consensus, greater rejection of conspiracies, greater acceptance of expert recommendations, and greater ability to distinguish fact from opinion than did individuals who reported voting for Trump, another candidate, or nonvoters.** Individuals who voted for Trump tended to resemble nonvoters or third-party voters on most Truth Decay measures, with the exception that Trump voters exhibited greater rejection of scientific consensus. **Which candidate an individual voted for in 2016 (Trump or Clinton) is generally a stronger predictor of resistance to Truth Decay than is political party (Democrat/Republican/independent) affiliation.**

Table 5.11 summarizes these results, focusing on the strongest statistical associations.

Principle Component Analysis of Truth Decay Indicators

These analyses assume that our a priori groupings of survey items meaningfully reflect how these items are interrelated in people's minds and in U.S. culture. For example, it is possible that endorsing conspiracy theories is strongly related to accepting recommendations of some experts but not of other experts. Many such rearrangements of the survey items can be specified that cut across our a priori scales of resistance/susceptibility to Truth Decay.

To assess the data in a manner that does not presume our original groupings, we examined the interrelationships among the 33 survey items relating to Truth Decay using PCA (Jolliffe, 2003). PCA is an exploratory data analysis technique that attempts to uncover the underlying dimensionality of the data, maximizing the amount of variation in the fewest number of uncorrelated dimensions (PCs). These components are new weighted averages of the original items, with weights determined by how correlated each item is with a given component. A strength of this approach is that it is determined entirely empirically from intercorrelations among the survey

TABLE 5.11

Summary of Significant Predictors of a Priori Scales of Resistance/Susceptibility to Truth Decay

Measure	Predictors of Resistance to Truth Decay	Predictors of Susceptibility to Truth Decay
Endorsement of scientific consensus	• Greater income • Clinton voter in 2016 • Greater numeracy • Greater scientific reasoning	• Hispanic • Black or other race, non-Hispanic • Evangelical, Pentecostal, or nondenominational Christian • Regular religious attendance • Trump voter in 2016 • Greater magical reasoning • Greater ingroup bias
Endorsement of verifiable facts	• Older adult • Higher income • Greater scientific reasoning	• Female • Greater magical reasoning • Greater ingroup bias
Rejection of false conspiracy theories	• Older adult • Greater income • Clinton voter in 2016 • Greater numeracy • Greater scientific reasoning • Greater ingroup bias	• Hispanic • Black, non-Hispanic • Regular religious attendance • Greater magical reasoning • Greater availability bias
Ability to distinguish fact from opinion	• Clinton voter in 2016 • Greater numeracy • Greater scientific reasoning • Greater ingroup bias	• Black, non-Hispanic
Willingness to accept expert recommendations	• Greater income • Democrat • Clinton voter in 2016 • Greater unjustified confidence • Greater availability bias	
Philosophical positivism versus skepticism	• Higher income	• Greater ingroup bias

NOTE: Variables included if p-value < 0.01.

items rather than by a priori assumptions. A second strength is that each component, as a weighted average of all 33 items, typically has greater reliability (as assessed by Cronbach alpha) than would scales that were based on a smaller number of items.

The pattern of shared variation observed in our indicators of resistance/ susceptibility to Truth Decay strongly suggests that just three components describe 32 percent of the original variation across the 33 variables. Percentages of variance explained by the first ten components were

- PC1 = 17 percent
- PC2 = 7.9 percent
- PC3 = 7.3 percent
- PC4 = 4.7 percent
- PC5 = 3.8 percent
- PC6 = 3.7 percent
- PC7 = 3.6 percent
- PC8 = 3.3 percent
- PC9 = 3.1 percent
- PC10 = 3.0 percent.

Although there are no hard rules for how many components to analyze as meaningful, a common practice is to focus on the components that clearly account for greater variance than is observed in the plateau of variance explained that always manifests from this method (and is seen from PC4 onward). PC1 through PC3 met this criterion.

Table 5.12 presents how each of the original items load on these first three PCs, color coded to show the range of items most positively loaded on a component (darker green) to most negatively loaded (darker red). PC1, which describes 17 percent of the total variation, appears to reflect overall acceptance of mainstream society's notions of when something is true, with high-scoring individuals tending to accept recommendations by society's secular experts (such as scientists, lawyers, and government officials), reject false conspiracy theories, endorse scientific consensus and at least some verifiable facts, and distinguish fact from opinion. Individuals scoring low on this axis tend not to accept recommendations by society's experts, endorse conspiracy theories, reject scientific consensus and verifiable fact, and confuse fact and opinion.

TABLE 5.12

The Three Major Components of Truth Decay

Truth Decay Scale	Survey Question	Loadings		
		PC1 (17%)[a]	PC2 (7.9%)	PC3 (7.3%)
Endorsement of scientific consensus	Universe began with Big Bang	0.25	0.03	−0.14
	Humans likely evolved	0.25	0.04	−0.17
	Genetically modified food safe	0.17	0.17	0.11
	Vaccines safe	0.21	0.14	0.14
	Homeopathic remedies ineffective	0.14	0.14	0.02
	Human contribution to rise in global temperature	0.21	−0.18	−0.25
Endorsement of verifiable facts	Violent crime in United States decreasing	0.23	0.15	−0.06
	Estimate of deaths in Puerto Rico resulting from Hurricane Maria is accurate	0.09	−0.06	−0.12
	U.S. drone strikes killed more combatants than innocents	−0.02	0.15	0.28
	More Jews than Muslims live in the United States	0.10	0.14	0.06
	Minority population will outnumber White population in 21–30 years (but not sooner)	0.06	0.07	0.03
Willingness to accept expert recommendations	Trust scientists	0.29	−0.14	0.01
	Trust doctors	0.23	−0.10	0.22
	Trust government officials	0.19	−0.29	0.21
	Trust business leaders	0.05	−0.21	0.45
	Trust religious leaders	−0.09	−0.15	0.45
	Trust journalists	0.26	−0.32	−0.04
	Trust lawyers	0.17	−0.27	0.23
	Trust scholars	0.24	−0.23	0.07

Table 5.12—Continued

		Loadings		
Truth Decay Scale	Survey Question	PC1 (17%)[a]	PC2 (7.9%)	PC3 (7.3%)
Rejection of false conspiracy theories	Reject 9/11 trutherism theory	0.15	0.33	0.22
	Reject Obama birtherism theory	0.26	0.00	−0.17
	Reject theory that moon landings were fake	0.18	0.34	0.10
	Reject JFK assassination conspiracy theory	0.21	0.20	0.09
	Reject theory that Elvis Presley and/or Tupac Shakur are not dead	0.17	0.24	0.01
Ability to distinguish fact from opinion	Fact: Undocumented immigrants have legal rights under U.S. constitution	0.13	0.03	−0.02
	Opinion: Government is always wasteful/inefficient	0.10	−0.04	−0.04
	Fact: Spending on Social Security and Medicare makes up the largest portion of the federal budget	0.10	0.14	0.09
	Opinion: $15 minimum wage is essential to the U.S. economy	0.01	0.23	0.16
	Opinion: Undocumented immigrants are a big problem	0.14	−0.10	−0.22
	Fact: U.S. health care costs are highest in world	0.12	0.05	0.01
Philosophical positivism versus skepticism	Scientific method best	0.25	0.01	−0.07
	Objective right/wrong	0.01	−0.05	0.11

NOTE: Statistics are loadings from an unrotated PCA. Darker green indicates more positive loading; white is near zero; darker red is more negative loading.

[a] Information in parentheses is the percentage variance described.

PC2 describes an additional 7.9 percent of the total variation not described by PC1 (Table 5.12). Loadings on PC2 are similar to PC1; the main difference is that individuals with high scores on PC2 are less willing to accept recommendations by societal experts and more philosophically skeptical of an objective standard of truth. Individuals who score low on PC2 accept recommendations by experts but rate poorly on all other features of resistance/susceptibility to Truth Decay.

PC3 explains an additional 7.3 percent of variation (Table 5.12). This component might be associated with partisanship, given the beliefs associated with each extreme. Those with higher values on this component believe that President Obama was born outside the United States, reject 9/11 as an inside job, reject evolution and global warming, and think vaccines and genetically modified food are safe (all self-reported). Individuals at the other end of this component, in contrast, believe 9/11 was an inside job and reject the notion that President Obama was born outside the United States. They believe in the Big Bang, evolution, and human contributions to the rise in global temperatures but think vaccines and genetically modified food are unsafe.

Predicting Truth Decay Principle Components

We proceeded with similar correlational and regression analyses for the Truth Decay PCs as we did for our a priori categorization of the Truth Decay survey items. In this next set of regressions, the outcome variables were the PC scores assigned to each individual on PC1, PC2, or PC3. These scores reflect weighted averages of an individual's original survey responses, with the weights reflected in the loadings on a given component. In this way, they reflect each individual's position on the inferred PC. By then analyzing the PCs as outcomes, we avoid the issue of a small number of items that entered into each of the a priori scales of resistance/susceptibility to Truth Decay. Each PC reflects a weighted average across the total set of Truth Decay survey items.

Table 5.13 presents bivariate correlations between the first three PCs and our main predictors of interest. This analysis is the same as the one that we conducted with our a priori scales of resistance/susceptibility to Truth Decay to examine descriptively the associations with resistance/susceptibility to

TABLE 5.13

Correlations Between Principal Component Measures of Truth Decay and Reasoning or Bias Measures

Measure of Reasoning or Cognitive Bias	PC1	PC2	PC3
Numeracy	0.38	0.31	0.04
Scientific reasoning	0.31	0.29	−0.03
Magical reasoning	−0.28	0.1	0.15
Availability bias	−0.18	−0.29	−0.01
Unjustified confidence	0.04	0	0.15
Ingroup bias	0	0	0.02

Truth Decay but without controlling for other variables in a multiple regression. The associations with PC1 follow a pattern similar to the a priori indicators; numeracy and scientific reasoning predict higher scores while magical reasoning (self-reported) and availability bias predict lower scores. The associations with PC2 are also similar to that of the earlier analysis; the exception is a positive correlation with magical reasoning (self-reported). The associations with PC3, on the other hand, are quite different; magical reasoning (self-reported) and unjustified confidence predict higher scores, but there are no strong relationships with any of the other reasoning or bias measures.

As noted in our earlier analysis, these bivariate correlations do not control for demographic and social variables, nor do they pit the cognitive processes against each other to assess relationships once others have their effects estimated. Thus, we first applied multiple linear regression analyses that included all cognitive variables in a single model for each of the three PCs (Table 5.14).

However, neither of these analyses control for the possibility that tendencies to certain reasoning processes or biases and resistance/susceptibility to Truth Decay might both be caused by other covariates. For example, a plausible hypothesis would be that some cognitive processes (such as scientific reasoning or magical thinking) and resistance/susceptibility to Truth Decay might all be learned separately (that is, they are not functionally linked in human minds) but are learned as part of socialization into particular demographic groups that tend to teach these items together. By controlling for

TABLE 5.14

Multiple Linear Regression of Principal Component Measures of Truth Decay on Biases and Reasoning Processes

Predictor Variable	Regression Coefficients (unstandardized) Outcome Variable		
	PC1	PC2	PC3
Measure of reasoning or cognitive bias			
Numeracy	0.29***	0.11***	0.004
Scientific reasoning	0.28***	0.20***	−0.06
Magical reasoning	−0.29***	−0.18***	0.06*
Availability bias	−0.49	−1.37***	−0.06
Unjustified confidence	0.06	0.01	0.13***
Ingroup bias	0.04	0.04	0.04
Law of small numbers	0.07	0.04	0.14
Constant	−2.11***	−0.42*	−0.76***
Overall model performance			
R^2	0.2	0.18	0.03
Adjusted R^2	0.2	0.18	0.03
Residual SE (df = 1,291)	2.11	1.46	1.52
F Statistic (df = 7; 1,291)	47.47***	40.60***	6.19***

NOTES: Responses of "unsure" have been recoded as the mean of an individual's responses to related questions. * $p < 0.05$; ** $p < 0.01$; *** $p < 0.001$. Sample size = 1,299.

demographic variables, we can better assess whether cognitive processes might have a reliable causal relationship with resistance/susceptibility to Truth Decay that is not merely an idiosyncratic outcome of the culture history of a particular demographic group. For example, people might believe in climate change because they are taught to reason scientifically and then use that reasoning capability to evaluate the evidence. However, they also might be taught by their social group to (1) believe in climate change and (2) reason scientifically, but they do not arrive at their climate change beliefs because they ever actually looked at the evidence. In this scenario, scientific reasoning and climate change beliefs are simply being coinherited by certain social groups (potentially, upper-class White Americans) but they are not causally linked to one another. Both are caused by idiosyncrasies of U.S. culture history. We applied a linear multiple regression that included both the cognitive variables and demographic controls as a way to net out the potential effects of how demographic groups might produce causally spurious statistical associations between cognitive variables and resistance/susceptibility to Truth Decay (Table 5.15).

Many of the reasoning and bias measures appeared statistically significant in the multiple regression to predict scores on PC1 that controls for the bias measures and for demographics. **Numeracy, scientific reasoning, and unjustified confidence all were positively associated with resistance to Truth Decay; the association with magical reasoning (self-reported) was negative.** The relationships with ingroup bias (self-reported) and availability bias were not significant in the multiple regression.

For PC2, ingroup bias (self-reported) and scientific reasoning were positively associated with resistance to Truth Decay; the association with magical reasoning and availability bias both were significantly negative. The association with ingroup bias is notable because this reflects a statistical association after already controlling for political party, voting behavior, and religiosity and religious affiliation (all of these variables were self-reported). Ingroup bias was measured via a set of questions, derived from the World Values Survey, that asked whether individuals would "mind" or "not mind" living next to someone of a different language, religion, race, or other characteristics. In the regression for PC2 as an outcome, ingroup bias appears associated with resistance to Truth Decay on PC2 after controlling for various social affiliations that one might assume would capture tendencies to favor an individual's cultural ingroup. This relationship of ingroup bias also does not derive from an association with accepting expert recommendations, because PC2 reflects resistance to Truth Decay generally but also systematic nonacceptance of expert recommendations, even those of business and religious leaders (Table 5.11). The older, Republican, White individuals who voted for Trump (self-reported) and who scored high on PC2 appear to have no trusted broker for truthful information despite their generally endorsing science and verifiable facts and rejecting false conspiracy theories.

TABLE 5.15

Linear Regression Predicting Principal Component Measures of Truth Decay

Predictor Variable	Regression Coefficients (unstandardized) Outcome Variable		
	PC1	PC2	PC3
Age	0.01	0.02***	−0.00004
Female	−0.06	−0.23**	−0.08
Education			
Less than high school	−0.39	−0.004	−0.12
Some college	−0.04	0.28*	−0.1
College degree	0.42*	0.33*	−0.05
Income midpoint/10,000	0.06***	0.01	0.02*
Race			
Hispanic (n = 148)	−0.47**	−0.69***	0.04
Black, non-Hispanic (n = 81)	−1.24***	−0.53**	−0.15
Asian, non-Hispanic (n = 33)	−0.96**	0.04	−0.03
Other, non-Hispanic (n = 26)	−1.24***	−0.005	−0.54*
Born in United States	−0.24	0.03	0.07
Religion			
Mainstream Protestant	−0.07	0.03	0.29*
Evangelical or Pentecostal	−0.21	−0.35	0.64***
Nondenominational Christian	−0.24	−0.14	0.27*
Other Christian groups	−0.06	0.31	0.16
Jewish	−0.13	−0.05	−0.26
Other religions	0.16	−0.48*	−0.63**
No religious affiliation	−0.18	−0.02	−0.40**
Atheist or agnostic	0.60**	0.25	−0.48**
Religious service attendance	−0.20***	−0.02	0.13***

Table 5.15—Continued

Predictor Variable	Regression Coefficients (unstandardized) Outcome Variable		
	PC1	PC2	PC3
Political affiliation			
Democrat	0.50***	−0.26*	0.11
Republican	−0.07	0.11	0.32**
Clinton voter in 2016	1.08***	−0.21	−0.002
Trump voter in 2016	−0.90***	0.52***	0.95***
Measure of reasoning or cognitive bias			
Numeracy	0.15***	0.06*	−0.01
Scientific reasoning	0.12**	0.21***	−0.01
Magical reasoning	−0.14***	−0.15***	−0.02
Availability bias	−0.29	−0.84***	0.37
Unjustified confidence	0.09**	−0.03	0.09***
Ingroup bias	−0.01	0.12***	0.02
Constant	−1.84***	−1.35***	−1.55***
Overall model performance			
R^2	0.52	0.35	0.3
Adjusted R^2	0.51	0.34	0.28
Residual SE (df = 1,266)	1.65	1.31	1.31
F Statistic (df = 30; 1,266)	45.79***	22.97***	17.85***

NOTES: Base levels: male, high school, non-Hispanic White, born outside the United States, Catholic, independent voting affiliation, voted for other candidate in 2016. Responses of "unsure" have been recoded as the mean of an individual's responses to related questions. * $p < 0.05$; ** $p < 0.01$; *** $p < 0.001$. Sample size = 1,297.

PC3, which at either end appears to reflect alternative partisan versions of susceptibility to Truth Decay (higher scores = conservative, lower scores = liberal), **exhibited a significant association with only unjustified confidence among the reasoning and bias measures. Greater unjustified confidence was associated on PC3 with greater susceptibility to liberal Truth Decay.**

Regarding the demographics that were added primarily as controls to assess the significance of the bias and reasoning measures, **those individuals who scored higher on PC1 tended to be more educated, have higher incomes, identify as non-Hispanic White, be less involved in formal religion, identify as Democrats, and be more likely to report voting for Clinton and less likely to report voting for Trump in 2016 relative to nonvoters and those who voted for other candidates (all self-reported).** These individuals also tended to score higher on numeracy and scientific reasoning and lower on magical reasoning while also displaying greater unjustified confidence.

Those scoring higher on PC2, in contrast, tended to be older, male, college educated, not identify as Black or Hispanic or as Democrats, and report having voted for Trump in 2016 (all self-reported). These individuals showed higher scientific reasoning skills (although not necessarily higher numeracy) and lower magical reasoning. They were less susceptible to availability bias, but more susceptible to ingroup bias. Scores on PC2 showed no significant associations with religious service attendance or affiliation.

As noted previously in Table 5.12, PC3 appears to be qualitatively different. **Those scoring higher tended to have higher incomes, identify as Christians and Republicans, and report having voted for Trump in 2016, whereas those scoring lower had lower incomes, identified as non-Christians and non-Republicans, and reported not voting for Trump in 2016 (all self-reported).**

Table 5.16 summarizes the most statistically significant of these relationships, in terms of whether they predict higher or lower scores on each PC.

Cultural Consensus Analysis of Truth Decay Indicators

The PCA relaxed our assumptions about how the survey items should be grouped together but retained our assumptions that each survey item

TABLE 5.16

Summary of Significant Predictors of Principal Component Measures of Truth Decay

Measure	Predictors of Higher Scores	Predictors of Lower Scores
PC1: Higher scores correspond to a priori assessment, using an external criterion of truth.	• Higher income • Democrat • Clinton voter in 2016 • Atheist or agnostic • Higher numeracy • Higher scientific reasoning • Higher unjustified confidence	• Non-White • Hispanic • More religious attendance • Trump voter in 2016 • Higher magical reasoning
PC2: Higher scores similar to PC1, but with greater distrust of experts.	• Older • Trump voter in 2016 • Higher scientific reasoning • Higher ingroup bias	• Female • Hispanic • Black, non-Hispanic • Higher magical reasoning • Higher availability bias
PC3: Higher scores correspond more with conservative partisanship; lower scores correspond more with liberal partisanship.	• Evangelical or Pentacostal • More religious attendance • Trump voter in 2016 • Higher unjustified confidence • Republican	• Other, atheist or agnostic, or no religious affiliation

NOTE: Variables included if p-value < 0.01.

reflected resistance to Truth Decay at one end of the spectrum and susceptibility to Truth Decay at the other. This assumption is reasonable because it reflects the judgment of a set of researchers who consulted published evidence-based literature when designing the items. It does, however, assume valid criteria for truth external to U.S. culture itself.

A different conceptualization of truth with respect to these items is the consensus of what "truth" is within U.S. culture. We can use the ALP responses to assess what most Americans answer about the items as the consensus viewpoint, which corresponds to the consensus model for knowledge as developed by anthropologists for the purpose of studying other cultures. Anthropologists wish to remain agnostic as to their own judgment about the truth of their informant's claims, but they recognize that some informants are more in tune with their culture's views on a topic than are others. They developed CCA as a method to address this conundrum (Romney, Weller, and Batchelder, 1986). CCA works in a manner similar to PCA, but instead of creating new components that reflect shared variance in the survey items, it develops new components to reflect shared agreement among the respondents. It can be performed by applying PCA to the transpose of the usual data matrix (Romney, Batchelder, and Weller, 1987; Weller, 2007). This means individuals are given a component loading score from –1 to 1 that reflects the correlation of their survey answers with the central tendency of answers across all respondents.

Intuitively, this reflects how much an individual's answers correspond to or deviate from the general cultural consensus. As an example, we asked in our survey whether the rate of violent crime in the United States was increasing or decreasing. Although objectively measured rates show that it is decreasing, the consensus of our respondents said that the rate of violent crime was increasing. In this case, the CCA would treat an answer of "increasing" as the accepted truth.

Anthropologists developed several guidelines for when the statistical assumptions of CCA are satisfied. One, which corresponds to whether consensus has been identified, is that the eigenvalue for the first CCA component should be more than three times greater than the second. In our CCA, the first eigenvalue was 16 times greater than the second. The first CCA component described 75 percent of variation among respondents; the second and third described 4.6 percent and 4.1 percent, respectively. Hence, a single-component "culture" of resistance to Truth Decay is supported by the CCA.

Another statistical guideline for a valid CCA is that the loadings for individuals generally range from 0 to 1 (that is, few negative loadings), with 0 reflecting an individual who is largely uninformed about their culture's beliefs and 1 reflecting an individual with a great deal of knowledge of their culture's beliefs. In this case, the "culture's beliefs" would be the typical views of the American population about Truth Decay items. The loadings from our CCA analysis were all greater than 0 and less than 1, which again supports the hypothesis that a consensus culture does exist for these items and among our sampled individuals.

The results reported in this section come from a consensus analysis that applies PCA to the transpose of the individual by belief matrix, which essentially extracts loadings that reflect agreement of each individual with the multivariate central tendency of answers across all other individuals and across all survey items (Romney, Batchelder, and Weller, 1987; Weller, 2007).

A more complex version of CCA would further transform interperson corre-lations to correct for chance agreement. When this transformation is done, the loadings for each individual are interpretable in a Bayesian context as the probability that the individual knows the correct response for their cul-ture. We performed the method more simply because our item scales vary from binary to five or six items, which makes correcting for chance agree-ment difficult as they come from different chance distributions.[3]

Drawing on this approach, we proceeded to extract the consensus view in our sample. This is a weighted average of the responses across all indi-viduals with the weights being their loading on CCA component 1. This consensus differs from the simple average across all individuals because it privileges information from those who the analysis has inferred to be more informed about their own culture's views on these items. Table 5.17 describes the general consensus as revealed by this analysis. The consen-sus view (third column) reports the weighted average of the responses; the scored item range (fourth column) reports the possible responses; and the external standard of truth (fifth column) presents the objective standard that was used in our previous analyses.

Table 5.17 makes it clear that several of the cultural consensus views on these items differ from the external truth criteria that we used to define them. Among the acceptance of expert recommendation questions, the consensus view accepts more than rejects recommendations only for sci-entists, medical doctors, and scholars of the humanities. Recommendations by other practitioners of public expertise and service, such as government and religious officials and journalists, all are more rejected than accepted (self-reported, score < 3).

---

[3] When a single chance distribution is not identifiable, researchers have recommended the simpler PCA be applied to the transposed data matrix because it easily accommo-dates data with scales where chance agreement is difficult or impossible to assess. For example, Romney, Batchelder, and Weller (1987) and Weller (2007) used this method for ranked data, calling it the "informal" method of CCA. By *informal*, they did not mean lacking in formal methodology; they meant that the PCA approach lacks a for-mally specified chance agreement and factor model underlying it. The interpretation of the informal CCA results are largely identical, but the loadings for individuals can no longer be interpreted as their probability of knowing correct answers; instead, the load-ings are merely a relative scoring of a respondent's cultural knowledge compared with the other individuals in the sample.

TABLE 5.17

Cultural Consensus View for Truth Decay Survey Items Compared with External Standard of Truth

A Priori Scales of Resistance/ Susceptibility to Truth Decay	Survey Item	Consensus View	Scored Item Range	External Standard of Truth
Endorsement of scientific consensus	Universe began with Big Bang	0.47	0, 1	1
	Humans likely evolved	0.51	0, 1	1
	Genetically modified food safe	0.34	0, 1	1
	Vaccines safe	0.83	0, 1	1
	Homeopathic remedies ineffective	0.41	0, 1	1
	Human contribution to rise in global temperature	0.72	0, 1	1
Endorsement of verifiable facts	Violent crime in United States decreasing	0.36	0, 1	1
	Estimate of deaths in Puerto Rico resulting from Hurricane Maria is accurate	0.67	0, 1	1
	U.S. drone strikes killed more combatants than innocents	0.40	0, 1	1
	More Jews than Muslims live in the United States	0.44	0, 1	1
	Minority population will outnumber White population in 21–30 years (but not sooner)	0.22	0, 1	1

70

Table 5.17—Continued

A Priori Scales of Resistance/ Susceptibility to Truth Decay	Survey Item	Consensus View	Scored Item Range	External Standard of Truth
Rejection of false conspiracy theories	Reject 9/11 trutherism theory	3.99	0–5	Higher
	Reject Obama birtherism theory	3.74	0–5	Higher
	Reject theory that moon landings were fake	4.38	0–5	Higher
	Reject JFK assassination conspiracy theory	2.61	0–5	Higher
	Reject theory that Elvis Presley and/or Tupac Shakur are not dead	4.53	0–5	Higher
Ability to distinguish fact from opinion	Fact: Undocumented immigrants have legal rights under U.S. constitution	0.72	0, 1	1
	Opinion: Government is always wasteful/inefficient	0.54	0, 1	1
	Fact: Spending on Social Security and Medicare makes up the largest portion of the federal budget	0.79	0, 1	1
	Opinion: $15 minimum wage is essential to the U.S. economy	0.69	0, 1	1
	Opinion: Undocumented immigrants are a big problem	0.66	0, 1	1
	Fact: U.S. health care costs are highest in world	0.89	0, 1	1

Table 5.17—Continued

A Priori Scales of Resistance/ Susceptibility to Truth Decay	Survey Item	Consensus View	Scored Item Range	External Standard of Truth
Willingness to accept expert recommendations	Trust scientists	4.42	0–6	Higher
	Trust doctors	4.52	0–6	Higher
	Trust government officials	2.54	0–6	Higher
	Trust business leaders	3.05	0–6	Higher
	Trust religious leaders	2.87	0–6	Higher
	Trust journalists	2.76	0–6	Higher
	Trust lawyers	3.08	0–6	Higher
	Trust scholars	3.93	0–6	Higher
Philosophical positivism versus skepticism	Scientific method best	3.79	0–5	Higher
	Objective right/wrong	3.53	0–5	Higher

The consensus view, however, rejects most conspiracy theories and endorses both philosophical positivism items. Despite the consensus view's trust of scientists, the endorsement of scientific consensus items are scattered across the break point (0.5) for the correct (1) and incorrect (0) answers as assessed by external evidence.

The items related to endorsing verifiable facts (self-reported) show the greatest divergence between the cultural consensus view and the externally defined truth view. These items were devised such that a 1 indicated a correct answer and a 0 indicated an incorrect answer, with *correctness* meaning the view that is most supported by empirical evidence readily available in the mainstream media. The cultural consensus view of these items is often substantially less than 0.5, meaning that most of the sample answered these items incorrectly. This result is perhaps consonant with the sample's low acceptance of recommendations by journalists, in that these verifiable fact items are news issues rather than scientific ones. It is not surprising that a public that does not accept what journalists say finds itself misinformed about journalistic information. We note that this effect might arise from individuals who, because they do not accept journalist recommendations, are perhaps not consuming news in the first place.

Those results contrast with the questions that focused on distinguishing fact from opinion. Here again, a 1 indicated a correct response using external definitions of truth, but the external definition is the formal definition of a factual statement versus an opinion statement in the Western tradition of formal logic–based rhetoric. Across most of these items, the consensus view among ALP respondents matched the view of formal rhetoric in that the consensus is generally substantially more than 0.5.

As in our prior analyses with Truth Decay scales and PCs, we can assess with the CCA how cognitive processes are associated with consensus truth (CCA component 1). The bivariate correlations of the reasoning processes and cognitive biases are shown in Table 5.18.

A multiple linear regression can be used to estimate effects for each reasoning process or cognitive bias after netting out the estimated effects for the others (Table 5.19.)

However, neither of these analyses control for the possibility that tendencies to certain reasoning processes or biases and resistance to Truth Decay might both be caused by other covariates. By controlling for demographic

TABLE 5.18

Correlations Between Cultural Consensus Measurement of Truth Decay and Reasoning or Bias Measures

Measure of Reasoning or Cognitive Bias	CCA Loading of Individuals
Numeracy	0.22
Scientific reasoning	0.13
Magical reasoning	−0.2
Availability bias	−0.1
Unjustified confidence	0.08
Ingroup bias	0.15

variables, we can better assess whether the cognitive processes might have a reliable causal relationship to resistance to Truth Decay that is not merely an idiosyncratic outcome of the culture history of particular demographic groups (Table 5.19). These estimates reflect the associations of these variables with the cultural consensus of what is "truth" as indicated by the survey respondents themselves rather than an externally defined set of facts and evidence. The outcome variable in the regression models was the loading for each individual on the first CCA component (Table 5.19).

The results of the regression with demographic covariates indicate that only greater ingroup bias (self-reported) and greater unjustified confidence are associated with resistance to Truth Decay in this analysis. Thus, by remaining agnostic to external scholarly standards for truth, the elements of greater scientific reasoning and numeracy and less magical reasoning are no longer significantly associated as they were in the previous analysis (Table 5.20). **This suggests that the consensus of truth, as adjudicated by the multivariate agreement among respondents themselves, does not significantly associate with the reasoning processes that are taught as correct by formal educational systems.** That is, consensus truth in our sample is uncorrelated with numeracy and scientific reasoning.

Those whose views on truth corresponded more closely to the cultural consensus tended to have higher household incomes, identify as White and as Democrats, and report having voted for Clinton in 2016

TABLE 5.19

Multiple Linear Regression for Cultural Consensus Measurement of Truth Decay and Reasoning or Bias Measures

Predictor Variable	Regression Coefficients (unstandardized) Outcome Variable CCA Loading of Individuals
Measure of reasoning or cognitive bias	
Numeracy	0.0004***
Scientific reasoning	0.0001
Magical reasoning	−0.0003**
Availability bias	−0.001
Unjustified confidence	0.0002**
Ingroup bias	0.001***
Law of small numbers	0.001*
Constant	0.02***
Overall model performance	
R^2	0.1
Adjusted R^2	0.09
Residual SE (df = 1,291)	0.005
F Statistic (df = 7; 1,291)	20.37***

NOTES: Responses of "unsure" have been recoded as the mean of an individual's responses to related questions. * $p < 0.05$; ** $p < 0.01$; *** $p < 0.001$. Sample size = 1,299.

(self-reported). There are no significant associations in either direction with religious service attendance or religious affiliation (self-reported). Strongly significant results across the bias or reasoning measures and demographics are summarized in Table 5.21.

In the section titled "Consensus Analysis Implementation with a Formal Model for Chance Answers" in Appendix C, we present a robustness check on these regression results, where we also conducted the "formal" CCA method that corrects for an assumed model of chance agreement. We did

TABLE 5.20

Multiple Linear Regression for Cultural Consensus Measurement of Truth Decay

Predictor Variable	Regression Coefficients (unstandardized) Outcome Variable CCA Loading of Individuals
Age	0.0002
Female	−0.0002
Education	
Less than high school	−0.02
Some college	−0.003
College degree	0.002
Income midpoint/10,000	0.001***
Race	
Black, non–Hispanic (n = 81)	−0.02***
Hispanic (n = 148)	−0.01
Asian (n = 33)	−0.02**
Other (n = 26)	−0.02**
Born in United States	−0.01
Religion	
Mainstream Protestant	0.003
Evangelical or Pentecostal	0.005
Nondenominational Christian	−0.0004
Other Christian groups	0.01
Jewish	−0.002
Other religions	−0.003
No religious affiliation	−0.01
Atheist or agnostic	0.005
Religious service attendance	−0.002

Table 5.20—Continued

Predictor Variable	Regression Coefficients (unstandardized) Outcome Variable CCA Loading of Individuals
Political affiliation	
Democrat	0.01***
Republican	0.002
Clinton voter in 2016	0.01***
Trump voter in 2016	−0.01
Measure of reasoning or cognitive bias	
Numeracy	0.002*
Scientific reasoning	−0.001
Magical reasoning	−0.001
Availability bias	−0.001
Unjustified confidence	0.002***
Ingroup bias	0.01***
Constant	0.23***
Overall model performance	
R^2	0.25
Adjusted R^2	0.23
Residual SE (df = 1,259)	0.04
F Statistic (df = 31; 1,259)	13.57***

NOTES: Responses of "unsure" have been recoded as the mean of an individual's responses to related questions. * $p < 0.05$; ** $p < 0.01$; *** $p < 0.001$. Sample size = 1,291.

this with the software UCINET (Borgatti, Everett, and Freeman, 2002). For this analysis, we dichotomized all the variables to enable them to be derived from a similar "chance" distribution. In accord with prior recommendations, we replaced any missing responses for individual items with a random selection for this analysis.

In our view, the formal method for these data is inappropriate because it assumes that answering any of the possible response options is equally likely,

TABLE 5.21

Summary of Significant Predictors of Agreement with the Cultural Consensus of Truth

Truth Decay Measure	Predictors of Views Closer to Cultural Consensus	Predictors of Views Further from Cultural Consensus
Cultural consensus views	• Higher income • Democrat • Clinton voter in 2016 • Greater unjustified confidence • Greater ingroup bias	• Black, Asian, or other race, Non-Hispanic

NOTE: Variables included if p-value < 0.01.

especially for individuals who opted out of a single item within a set. The items were not constructed, however, to have this property, which is why we prefer the informal method articulated by Weller (2007). Furthermore, in the analyses reported in this chapter, we replaced missing values with an individual's own mean response from the other related items (for example, the other conspiracy theories, the other items related to endorsement of scientific consensus). By doing this, we avoided creating a false central tendency in the CCA that would occur had we reset missing values to the center of the scale. By replacing with the self-mean, we do not at all alter the mean response for each individual, thus not altering the multivariate central tendency.

Random replacement, in contrast, inserts variance that, for our data, is most certainly generated from a distribution different than what generated the empirical data. These caveats being made, we did perform the formal CCA in UCINET for readers who are familiar with this method by using the random replacement.

In this formal CCA, the ratio of the first to second eigenvalue was 3.54, and there were 9 negative loadings out of 1,327 total loadings. Although, in theory, no loadings would be negative, the preponderance of results from this formal analysis still indicate evidence for a culture of Truth Decay.

The results from the CCA could be interpreted to indicate that individuals who are minorities within the ALP (that is, low income, non-White individuals who are not Democrats or Clinton voters [all self-reported]) merely have different views than do the majority White and middle- or upper-income panelists but that such differences in view are unrelated to

resistance/susceptibility to Truth Decay as externally defined. However, the demographic patterns in the regression of CCA loadings were substantively similar to those for prior regressions, which retained the externally defined orientation to truth. Thus, these demographic patterns appear to reflect real trends rather than an artifact of sampling.

As a further robustness check on these results, we repeated the CCA using only the 82 Black Americans in the sample. We did this because, in the CCA of the full sample, White respondents are a majority, which could overwhelm the statistical signal and prevent us from finding a distinctively Black American CCA cultural structure for these items. Our replication within the Black-only sample, however, refutes the idea that Black Americans have a different cultural structure for these items. The first component axis of the Black-only CCA described 73 percent of the variation; the second and third described 5.6 percent and 3.8 percent, respectively. These values were 75 percent, 4.6 percent, and 4.1 percent in the full sample. All the loadings were positive for individuals. The Pearson correlation of the loadings assigned to the 82 individuals from the Black-only CCA compared with their values from the full sample was 0.98. The correlation of the scores assigned for the variables for the Black-only CCA compared with the full-sample CCA was 0.97. In short, every metric from this analysis supports that Black and White Americans share a single common culture in terms of how they view the material we used in this survey.

As we noted early in this report, it would still be possible for bias to occur from the inclusion of items themselves. That is, we do not know what we did not ask in our survey. Perhaps there exists some other set of survey items that is pertinent to resistance/susceptibility to Truth Decay that would distinguish separate Black and White cultures. Given that most of our items came from previously published work, this potential bias would be institutional and apply more broadly than to just our study. We consider this matter a suitable subject for further research.

CHAPTER SIX

Discussion

Our study examined cognitive processes and cognitive biases as one of the proposed drivers of Truth Decay. To assess this relationship, we first developed a comprehensive assessment of three of the four trends of Truth Decay identified in prior research: heightened disagreement about facts and analytical interpretations of facts and data, blurring of the line between opinion and fact, and diminished trust in formerly respected institutions as sources of factual information.[1] This assessment includes six measures:

1. endorsement of scientific consensus
2. endorsement of verifiable facts
3. rejection of false conspiracy theories
4. ability to distinguish fact from opinion
5. willingness to accept expert recommendations
6. philosophical positivism **versus skepticism** (philosophy on truth).

To our knowledge, this is the first assessment of its kind. For that reason, the full instrument is included in Appendix A. We also retained the full item set rather than selecting better-performing items—a task left for future research. We fielded this instrument to a nationally representative sample of U.S. adults participating in the ALP. The survey also included measures of reasoning and cognitive biases, systematically selected for **potential relevance to Truth Decay.**

---

[1] The fourth trend, an increase in the relative volume and influence of opinion and personal experience over fact, is more an aspect of the environment in which people access information, and so was not addressed in this study.

These measures of resistance/susceptibility to Truth Decay were substantially and positively intercorrelated, consistent with there being a common underlying construct. Generally speaking, higher scores on the six scales were consistently predicted by greater numeracy, greater scientific reasoning, and less magical reasoning, consistent with our primary hypothesis. Among the cognitive biases, susceptibility to availability bias (a tendency to see more-memorable events as more likely) was associated with greater susceptibility to false conspiracy theories and with greater acceptance of recommendations by experts. Greater acceptance of expert recommendations also was associated with individuals displaying unjustified confidence in their knowledge. Ingroup bias (a discomfort with people from different social groups) was at times associated with greater susceptibility to Truth Decay (lower endorsement of scientific consensus and verifiable fact, less positivist philosophy) and at other times associated with greater resistance to Truth Decay (rejection of false conspiracy theories, ability to distinguish fact from opinion).

Recognizing that the list of Truth Decay indicators reflects an a priori assumption of how Truth Decay is organized, we also submitted all 33 individual items to an exploratory PCA, which detected three substantial dimensions explaining the variability in the items. **Notably, 17 percent of the variance in the Truth Decay indicators is accounted for by a single dimension, which corresponded fairly strongly with endorsement of scientific consensus, rejection of false conspiracy theories, and willingness to accept recommendations or information from experts, with somewhat weaker positive associations with endorsement of verifiable fact and ability to distinguish fact from opinion.** This component of resistance/susceptibility to Truth Decay was associated with greater numerical and scientific reasoning and lower magical reasoning. Hence, this first component corresponds most closely to what we a priori considered to be resistance to Truth Decay—a secular scientific truth. Among demographic controls, it was associated with being White, Democratic, and less religious.

A strong secondary component also appeared to capture somewhat informed respondents, but those who were more skeptical of experts. Individuals who scored high on this dimension generally disbelieve conspiracy theories. They endorse some scientific consensus items and verifiable facts, but only when those accord with conservative political stances.

For example, they believe vaccines and genetically modified food are safe but that human activity does not contribute to rising global temperatures and are ambivalent about the Big Bang and evolution. High scorers get at least some verifiable facts correct and show some ability to distinguish fact from opinion but tend to incorrectly believe it is a fact (rather than an opinion) that illegal immigrants are a big problem. Higher scorers on this dimension tend to have greater scientific reasoning and less availability bias and less magical reasoning. They also have greater ingroup bias. Among demographic controls, they tend to be older, identify as White or Asian and as Republican or independent, and report that they are not particularly religious or nonreligious. Considered all together, this component appears to measure agreement or disagreement with a truth-informed conservatism that is yet highly skeptical of recommendations by societal experts.

The third component appears to reflect a spectrum with alternative partisan positions on the issues on each end. The high end is conservative partisan (for example, those who accept recommendations of business and religious leaders most, reject 9/11 trutherism, endorse Obama birtherism, reject evolution, believe genetically modified food is safe). The low end, in contrast, is liberal partisan (for example, those who accept recommendations of scientists most and those of business and religious leaders least, endorse 9/11 trutherism, reject Obama birtherism, endorse evolution, believe genetically modified food is unsafe). Consistent with this interpretation, the most important demographic associations are with religious affiliation (Evangelical on one end, no religion or atheist or agnostic on the other), religious service attendance, political party, and reported 2016 presidential voting for Clinton. Also consistent with this interpretation that both ends of the scale equally reflect susceptibility to Truth Decay (but alternative partisan versions of it), the reasoning and bias measures are not especially associated with either end of the scale.

Finally, we conducted a cultural consensus analysis to provide a further robustness check on these interpretations. This analysis relaxes the assumption of an external scholarly standard for truth. Instead, it identifies the consensus view among respondents. This analysis largely replicates the previous analysis, but with loss of significance for some variables. Those respondents whose views are most consistent with the cultural consensus tend to have higher household incomes and to identify as non-Hispanic White and Democratic. They tend to be more numerate, but also display greater ingroup bias.

Scientific Implications

This is the first study of which we are aware to propose a comprehensive assessment of resistance/susceptibility to Truth Decay.[2] The six-measure assessment addresses three of the four trends defining Truth Decay (Kavanagh and Rich, 2018), providing a multifaceted view that can be examined for its individual components (as we did in our first set of regressions) or more holistically (as in our second and third sets of regressions). The fact that these six measures intercorrelate positively is consistent with there being an underlying construct of Truth Decay (or, alternately, a set of mutually reinforcing constructs), and construct validity is further supported by associations with measures of reasoning, notably numeracy, scientific reasoning, and magical reasoning. Availability and refinement of this assessment will facilitate future scientific studies of the causes and consequences of Truth Decay.

This study also provides the first, exploratory attempt at an individual-differences measure of susceptibility to availability bias. Such a measure fits within and provides an additional tool for the emerging literature on individual differences in decisionmaking competence (Bruine de Bruin, Parker, and Fischhoff, 2007; Parker et al., 2018), which has been associated with real-world life decision outcomes (Parker, Bruine de Bruin, and Fischhoff, 2015) and with individual differences in rationality (Stanovich and West, 2000; Stanovich, West, and Toplak, 2016).

These measures will need to undergo further development, as we learned a good deal from this first fielding. For example, the a priori scales of resistance/susceptibility to Truth Decay likely had too few items to be reliable indicators in themselves. The PCA results avoid this issue by leveraging all the Truth Decay items in each component score, but isolation of the initially proposed dimensions of the Truth Decay phenomenon could require

---

[2] The Comprehensive Assessment of Rational Thought inventory (Stanovich, West, and Toplak, 2016) offers assessments that are similar to but much longer than our scales for both rejection of false conspiracy theories and availability bias.

more extensive subscales. Item refinement, trimming items with low correlation with the overall measure, and development of new items could each contribute to this process, with future studies providing more accurate and efficient assessments. That the results were generally in line with our expectations suggests the value of future investment in this line of research.

At least some findings from the regression models were robust, however, to three very different specifications of the outcome variables (a priori scales of resistance/susceptibility to Truth Decay, PC scores from the Truth Decay survey items, and individuals' agreement with the consensus belief about these items). This suggests that our Truth Decay measures have some degree of nomological validity, meaning that they correlate in expected ways with other variables not used to create them (Nunnally and Bernstein, 1994).

Although our primary research interest was the potential role of cognitive processes in the Truth Decay phenomenon, the empirical results of this study frequently found demographic characteristics were more predictive of resistance/susceptibility to Truth Decay than were cognitive biases or reasoning processes. These results contradict interpretations that non-White or lower-income Americans would have less resistance to Truth Decay as a result of cognitive differences between them and higher-income White Americans. If such processes were happening, then our models should have found no effect of race or income on resistance/susceptibility to Truth Decay after controlling for reasoning processes and cognitive biases, because the hypothesized process would be that racial differences in cognition drive the differences in resistance/susceptibility to Truth Decay. We did not find this result; instead, racial and income differences frequently are significant after controlling for observable variation in cognition. This suggests that different cultural histories within U.S. society might account for resistance/susceptibility to Truth Decay more so than individual-level variation in reasoning processes or cognitive biases. This empirical finding then drove some of our implications for policy.

Policy Implications

Among the biases or reasoning processes, the most consistent finding across models was that increased numeracy and scientific reasoning and lower magical reasoning were associated with greater resistance to Truth Decay. Truth Decay resistance/susceptibility showed less relationship to cognitive biases that are thought to trigger short-term reactions. Thus, we did not find strong associations of Truth Decay resistance/susceptibility with the kinds of "tricks" known to be used by advertisers (for example, availability bias, unjustified confidence). Rather, the greatest predictors we found for Truth Decay resistance/susceptibility were reasoning processes that are developed over an individual's lifetime and likely are all at least somewhat adaptive within their proper context.

This suggests that potentially powerful tools to combat Truth Decay might reside within the educational system (conceived broadly) rather than in trying to counter biases such as availability bias and other biases related to "fast thinking" cognitive heuristics (Kahneman, 2011). Instead, society needs to be developing better informed and critically thinking citizens who can appropriately process the rapid media environments in which we all now must operate. However, we note that formal educational attainment (for example, high school diploma, college degree) was rarely associated with resistance to Truth Decay in any of the regression models. Only college degree–level education was slightly associated with some of the PCA models. This suggests that traditional education has provided limited leverage, beyond the concepts included in the model. Further examination of this lack of an effect could shed light on other, more productive developmental strategies.

A concerning finding across our models was that minority (non-White) respondents were more susceptible to Truth Decay. Although sometimes race was not significant, it often was, and there was not a single analysis in which non-White respondents scored as more resistant than White respondents to Truth Decay, after controlling for other variables, such as education, political party, and biases or reasoning processes. **This finding potentially reflects deep distrust of traditional sources of factual information among groups that have at times been systematically persecuted by societal institutions. The findings underscore the need for ongoing and open conversations about truth with all demographic groups in the United States.**

This observation about minorities has been noted in previous studies (Uscinski and Parent, 2014; Westergaard et al., 2014; Bogart et al., 2021), all of which indicate that this condition is unlikely to be a direct cause of any single cognitive process, such as myside bias. Minorities are thought to be more disposed to believe conspiracy theories because they have at times been victims of actual conspiracies (for example, the Tuskegee syphilis experiments on Black men and the World War II internment of Japanese Americans). This is potentially quite rational cognition. A similar process might occur with low-income, rural, White Americans (especially in the Southeast), who, in contrast to notions of the "American Dream," experience lower social mobility and consequently higher multigenerational poverty than seen in nearly any other developed country (Alesina, Glaeser, and Sacerdote, 2011; Reeves and Krause, 2018). Again, distrust of the establishment by members of such a group would not be myside bias per se but could be a rational conclusion derived from observing that the establishment does not help them. Further research is needed to disentangle the various cognitive, cultural, or historical processes that might account for the correlations we observed between resistance/susceptibility to Truth Decay and demographic variables.

Our models also support the assertion that the perceptions of key issues, worldviews, and even ways of processing information in the United States could also be split according to partisanship and religiosity. It appears that, by controlling for these variables in a multiple regression, we eliminated the significance for many of the reasoning processes and biases in the bivariate correlations. Assuming the cross-sectional regression is picking up on the most important variables, combating Truth Decay might be just as much a matter of somehow bridging the partisan politics of U.S. society as addressing cognitive processes.

The PCA, in which we relaxed our assumptions about which variables go together in categories, did extract a component for greater resistance to Truth Decay that was associated with Trump voters (component 2). This component, however, explained only one-half of the variance of the largest PC for Truth Decay, on which Trump voters were significantly less resistant to Truth Decay. Also, although individuals who scored high on component 2 generally endorsed science, rejected conspiracies, and distinguished fact from opinion, they tended to reject recommendations from any and all societal experts, even religious and business leaders. Put another way, component 2 is associated with distrust of all forms of societal experts, even traditional authorities within Republicanism, such as religious and business leaders. **In short, although one of the multivariate dimensions of resistance to Truth Decay was associated with Republicans and Trump voters, it simultaneously was also associated with low acceptance of recommendations by every form of recognized societal expert who could broker epistemic engagement with these individuals.**

Overall, the results point to a substantial disconnect between generally accepted truth and the beliefs of those who voted for Trump in 2016. Their skepticism of recommendations by all forms of societal experts makes it difficult to identify any traditional trusted messenger who would be credible to reestablish truth claims with this part of the American public. This highlights a substantial barrier to identifying common factual grounds on which to generate widespread support for many policy solutions. **A first task for policymakers for certain demographics of U.S. society is to reestablish trusted messengers for information. Strategies to disseminate accurate information through trusted messengers can only be followed once trusted messengers have been established.**

Limitations

This study has several limitations worth noting. First, the results presented here come from a single, cross-sectional, and largely exploratory survey, so we cannot draw causal conclusions. The results are consistent with and provide a first step in supporting the conceptual framework suggested by Kavanagh and Rich (2018), which includes cognitive processes and biases as a driver of Truth Decay. Future studies, however, should employ refined measures and stronger causal methods, such as experimental techniques involving informational primes and behavioral tasks. More naturalistic, real-world experiments would, of course, need to take into account ethical considerations of manipulating Truth Decay or its drivers. That said, the results suggest the promise of pursuing causal inquiries.

Second, as a survey-based study, we often relied on respondents' self-reports (for example, for endorsement or rejection of conspiracy theories), which can be biased if respondents are unable or unwilling to provide accurate answers. That said, many of the measures used here were performance measures with right and wrong answers and thus less susceptible to self-report biases. Ultimately, the potential limitations stemming from self-reporting should be addressed in future studies with behavioral outcomes.

Third, the results also depend on the recruited sample of respondents and its correspondence to the larger population of interest—U.S. adults. The ALP uses probability-sampling techniques to recruit participants, which alleviates many concerns associated with opt-in or convenience-sampled panels or with online crowd-sourcing recruitment services (Kennedy et al., 2020). We also employed sampling weights to better align the ALP sample with the U.S. adult population. That said, online panels typically have limited representation of certain underrepresented groups, such as non-White respondents and those with lower incomes or education, and the ALP is no exception. Future studies should attempt to replicate these results with other, diverse samples.

Fourth, the cognitive processes and biases examined here were carefully selected for their potential relevance to Truth Decay. That said, to keep survey length manageable, we limited both measure length (that is, the number of items per bias) and number of processes or biases we were able to assess. Some clearly relevant biases, such as myside bias (and the related concepts of confirmation bias and motivated reasoning), are not easily assessed using short online surveys. Given that demographics were quite predictive of Truth Decay, myside bias might account for some of the associations with demographics, but it also might not—thus, these results should be interpreted cautiously.

On one hand, some responses might not be the result of individual susceptibility to Truth Decay in a more general sense; rather they might be considered statements of social membership or myside bias. These individuals might see evidence on a given topic and either reject it because it does not match their preexisting belief or misinterpret it to fit their belief. But that is not the only possible pathway.

For example, we found that self-reported Democrats and those who self-reported as less religious are more likely than self-reported Republicans and more-religious respondents to accept evolution. That could occur through myside bias, which would mean the latter group of respondents adopts or endorses a belief against evolution for some reason *not having to do with interpretation of evidence* (perhaps through simple cultural copying) and then misinterprets facts and evidence in order to maintain this belief. Many other processes could account for this association, however. For example, education in the schools and homes of Republican respondents and religious respondents (self-reported) might not provide these individuals with the facts about natural history that make for compelling evidence of evolution. Thus, having never been exposed to the clear evidence for evolution, some of these respondents might logically disbelieve it. Then, when researchers conduct surveys with these respondents, they find these individuals misperceive evidence about evolution, but this misperception is a cause of their disbelief in evolution, not a result of it. That causal pathway is not myside bias, which occurs when a committed belief induces a misinterpretation of evidence, and not when the misinterpretation induces a belief.

That said, regardless of the causal pathway for a given individual, the expression of such beliefs has potential social ramifications for knowledge in other people. Those without an understanding of the scientific evidence might look to others in their social circles for signals of truth, resulting in the spread of false beliefs and the proliferation of Truth Decay, irrespective of whether false beliefs at an individual level result from poor evidence or emerge despite it.

Finally, and as already noted, the bias measures often displayed limited reliability. In many cases, this could be because of the shortness of the scales. For the assessment of Truth Decay, this is partially addressed through our examination of PCs as summary measures, as they are weighted averages of all 33 Truth Decay items. Future studies could employ already standardized but much longer assessments, such as the Adult Decision-Making Competence battery (Bruine de Bruin, Parker, and Fischhoff, 2007) or the CART (Stanovich, West, and Toplak, 2016), but trade-offs between reliable measurement and length of surveys, especially when multiple constructs are of interest, can often be difficult. Some of the measures, such as the Scientific Reasoning Scale (Drummond and Fischhoff, 2017) performed well as predictors, even with limited items, suggesting even stronger potential effects with the full scale.

Future Directions and Conclusions

In this report, we provide a first demonstration of the potential impact of cognitive processes and cognitive biases on three of the four trends defining Truth Decay. This generally supports the conceptual framework proposed by Kavanagh and Rich (2018). As noted, future work should replicate and extend these findings to other diverse samples (such as extensions to other countries), and use refined and additional measures and research designs more appropriate for establishing causality. That said, the findings here suggest the importance of developing informed and critically thinking citizens. Our result that resistance/susceptibility to Truth Decay was more related to reasoning processes developed over a person's life-span suggests that educational interventions might be critical to combating Truth Decay. Such interventions could include those promoting numeracy and scientific reasoning, and education on the appropriate epistemic contexts for religious and magical reasoning. Generally speaking, we did not find strong associations between resistance/susceptibility to Truth Decay and cognitive biases that arise from fast-thinking heuristics. The results further suggest that addressing those social processes is critical to combating Truth Decay; sociodemographic variables were consistently associated with resistance to Truth Decay. Addressing social processes should include addressing potential distrust among disadvantaged populations of traditional sources of factual information and combating what appear to be partisan divides in how Americans think about truth and evidence.

Survey Questions

The survey was administered from February 26 through March 13, 2019. Several demographic characteristics, such as age, gender, education, household income, race or ethnicity, and U.S. nativity, are collected regularly as part of management of the ALP, and come pre-merged with the survey data set. The political variables came from ALP presidential election surveys fielded in 2016. The sections that follow provide verbatim question wording for each of the measures used in our analyses but are organized by construct for presentational purposes. Notes are displayed in brackets. For questions with a correct answer, that answer is identified by an asterisk. Several biases, such as framing and law of small numbers, were assessed with only single items (or item pairs, in the case of framing) and were included only for exploratory purposes. These items, as we note, were not included in our analyses. The survey included these questions in the following order:

1. availability bias
2. first half of each framing question pair [excluded from analysis]
3. magical reasoning
4. ingroup bias
5. numeracy
6. law of small numbers [excluded from analysis]
7. unjustified confidence
8. scientific reasoning
9. endorsement of scientific consensus
10. willingness to accept expert recommendations
11. endorsement of verifiable facts
12. rejection of false conspiracy theories

13. two single items assessing agreement with (a) the scientific method being the best way we have for understanding the natural world, and (b) whether there are objective standards for right and wrong (i.e., philosophical positivism versus skepticism)
14. second half of each framing question pair [excluded from analysis]
15. ability to distinguish fact from opinion
16. religious affiliation and attendance of religious services.

The full survey instrument and data can be accessed at the American Life Panel data pages (RAND Corporation, undated).

Availability Bias

The first set of questions asks you to judge which of two events happens to more people in the U.S.

In a typical year, are more people in the U.S. attacked by sharks or killed by lightning?
- Attacked by sharks (1)
- Killed by lightning (2)*

In a typical year, is a person in the U.S. more likely to be struck by lightning or to win the Powerball lottery?
- Struck by lightning (1)*
- Win the Powerball lottery (2)

In a typical year, do more people in the U.S. die from suicide or homicide?
- Suicide (1)*
- Homicide (2)

In a typical year, do more people in the U.S. die from falls on stairs or storms (including hurricanes and tornadoes)?
- Falls on stairs (1)*
- Storms (including hurricanes and tornadoes) (2)

In the U.S., are there more physicians or post-secondary teachers (for example, college professors)?

- Physicians (1)
- Post-secondary teachers (2)*

In a typical year, do more people in the U.S. die from motor vehicle accidents or poisoning?

- Motor vehicle accidents (1)
- Poisoning (2)*

Framing

[These are two items selected from the Resistance to Framing subscale of the Adult Decision-Making Competence battery (Bruine de Bruin, Parker, and Fischhoff, 2007). These represent the first question in each pair. Because only single pairs were used for each of two types of framing, these items were only considered for exploratory purposes and not included in analyses.]

Imagine that recent evidence has shown that a pesticide is threatening the lives of 1,200 endangered animals. Two response options have been suggested:

If Option A is used, 600 animals will be saved for sure.

If Option B is used, there is a 75% chance that 800 animals will be saved, and a 25% chance that no animals will be saved.

Which option would you recommend to use?

- 1 Definitely would choose A (1)
- 2 (2)
- 3 (3)
- 4 (4)
- 5 (5)
- 6 Definitely would choose B (6)

Imagine the following situation. You are entertaining a special friend by inviting them for dinner. You are making your favorite lasagna dish with ground beef. Your roommate goes to the grocery store and purchases a package of ground beef for you. The label says 20% fat ground beef.

What's your evaluation of the quality of this ground beef?

- 1 Very low (1)
- 2 (2)
- 3 (3)
- 4 (4)
- 5 (5)
- 6 Very high (6)

[The next two items are the second questions in each pair and represent the counterpart to the two questions above.]

Please answer the following two questions using the numerical scales below.

Imagine that recent evidence has shown that a pesticide is threatening the lives of 1,200 endangered animals. Two response options have been suggested:

If Option A is used, 600 animals will be lost for sure.

If Option B is used, there is a 75% chance that 400 animals will be lost, and a 25% chance that 1,200 animals will be lost.

Which option do you recommend to use?

- 1 Definitely would choose A (1)
- 2 (2)
- 3 (3)
- 4 (4)
- 5 (5)
- 6 Definitely would choose B (6)

Imagine the following situation. You are entertaining a special friend by inviting them for dinner. You are making your favorite lasagna dish with ground beef. Your roommate goes to the grocery store and purchases a package of ground beef for you. The label says 80% lean ground beef.

What's your evaluation of the quality of this ground beef?

- 1 Very low (1)
- 2 (2)
- 3 (3)
- 4 (4)
- 5 (5)
- 6 Very high (6)

Magical Reasoning

[The following seven items were modified from an instrument published by Kingdon, Egan, and Rees (2012).]

Please indicate your level of agreement or disagreement with the following items.

I have a little ritual or superstition I do for my favorite sports team, like wearing a certain shirt or sitting in a particular chair.

- 0 Strongly disagree (0)
- 1 (1)
- 2 (2)
- 3 (3)
- 4 (4)
- 5 Strongly agree (5)
- Unsure (6)

Sometimes there can be connections between everyday events that we don't fully understand.
- 0 Strongly disagree (0)
- 1 (1)
- 2 (2)
- 3 (3)
- 4 (4)
- 5 Strongly agree (5)
- Unsure (6)

I would feel uncomfortable buying a house where a murder had occurred.
- 0 Strongly disagree (0)
- 1 (1)
- 2 (2)
- 3 (3)
- 4 (4)
- 5 Strongly agree (5)
- Unsure (6)

I avoid thinking or saying things that I think might jinx an outcome I want.
- 0 Strongly disagree (0)
- 1 (1)
- 2 (2)
- 3 (3)
- 4 (4)
- 5 Strongly agree (5)
- Unsure (6)

Some ancient peoples may have known secrets about the universe that we don't know today.
- 0 Strongly disagree (0)
- 1 (1)
- 2 (2)
- 3 (3)
- 4 (4)
- 5 Strongly agree (5)
- Unsure (6)

I think sometimes things really happen for a reason.
- 0 Strongly disagree (0)
- 1 (1)
- 2 (2)
- 3 (3)
- 4 (4)
- 5 Strongly agree (5)
- Unsure (6)

I have sometimes sensed an evil presence in a specific place where I was, like a particular room in a house.
- 0 Strongly disagree (0)
- 1 (1)
- 2 (2)
- 3 (3)
- 4 (4)
- 5 Strongly agree (5)
- Unsure (6)

Ingroup Bias

[These items come from the World Values Survey (Inglehart and Baker, 2000; Inglehart and Welzel, 2010).]

On this list are various groups of people. Please indicate any that you would not like to have as neighbors.

	Would not like (1)	Would not mind (2)
Drug addicts (1)		
People of a different race (2)		
People who have AIDS (3)		
Immigrants or foreign workers (4)		
People who are Lesbian, Gay, Bisexual, or Transgender (5)		
People of a different religion (6)		
Heavy drinkers (7)		
Unmarried couples living together (8)		
People who speak a different language (9)		
People of different political views (10)		

Numeracy

[The eight numeracy items were published by Weller et al. (2013), and are not reproduced here at request from the authors.]

Law of Small Numbers

[This item was included for exploratory purposes and not included in analyses.]

A certain town is served by two hospitals. In the larger hospital, about 45 babies are born each day; in the smaller hospital, about 15 babies are born each day. As you know, about 50% of all babies are boys. The exact percentage of baby boys, however, varies from day to day. Sometimes it may be higher than 50%, sometimes lower. For a period of one year, each hospital recorded the days on which more than 60% of the babies born were boys. Which hospital do you think recorded more such days?
- Larger hospital (1)
- Smaller hospital (2)*

Unjustified Confidence

Considering the nine questions involving numbers that you just answered, how many do you think you got correct?

[The nine items referenced here are the eight numeracy items and the one law of small numbers item, which was used only for purpose of comparison with this question. We also asked the following question, which was not used in the analysis:]

Considering the nine questions involving numbers that you just answered, what percent of ALP panelists do you think you scored better than?

Scientific Reasoning

[The following four questions were selected, after conversation with the primary author (Drummond), from the scale published by Drummond and Fischhoff (2017).]

Please select the correct answer for the following questions from the options provided. If you are not certain, please provide your best assessment.

A researcher has subjects put together a jigsaw puzzle either in a cold room with a loud radio or in a warm room with no radio. Subjects solve the puzzle more quickly in the warm room with no radio.

True or False? The scientist cannot tell if the radio caused subjects to solve the puzzle more slowly.

- True (1)*
- False (2)

A researcher has a group of subjects play a competitive game. Each subject's goal is to make money by buying and selling tokens. Subjects are paid a flat fee for participating in the experiment.

True or False? The researcher can confidently state that the behavior in the experiment reflects real-life buying and selling behavior.

- True (1)
- False (2)*

Subjects in an experiment must press a button whenever a blue dot flashes on their computer screen. At first, the task is easy for subjects. But as they continue to perform the task, they make more and more errors.

True or False? The blue dot must flash more quickly as the task progresses.

- True (1)
- False (2)*

A researcher develops a new method for measuring the surface tension of liquids. This method is more consistent than the old method.

True or False? The new method must also be more accurate than the old method.

- True (1)
- False (2)*

Endorsement of Scientific Consensus

How likely do you think it is that the universe began with the Big Bang?
- Very likely (1)
- Likely (2)
- Equally likely or unlikely (3)
- Unlikely (4)
- Very unlikely (5)

How likely do you think it is that humans evolved from another species of animal?
- Very likely (1)
- Likely (2)
- Equally likely or unlikely (3)
- Unlikely (4)
- Very unlikely (5)

In general, how safe do you think genetically modified foods are for human consumption?
- Very safe (1)
- Somewhat safe (2)
- Equally safe or unsafe (3)
- Somewhat unsafe (4)
- Very unsafe (5)

In general, how safe do you think vaccines are?
- Very safe (1)
- Somewhat safe (2)
- Equally safe or unsafe (3)
- Somewhat unsafe (4)
- Very unsafe (5)

In general, do you think homeopathic remedies are effective for treating illness?

Homeopathic remedies are characterized by the following: Medicine can cure a sick person if it can cause a similar sickness in a healthy person. The lower the dose of the medication, the greater its effectiveness.
- Very effective (1)
- Somewhat effective (2)
- Equally effective or ineffective (3)
- Somewhat ineffective (4)
- Very ineffective (5)

How likely do you think it is that human activities have contributed to the recent rise in global temperature?
- Very likely (1)
- Likely (2)
- Equally likely or unlikely (3)
- Unlikely (4)
- Very unlikely (5)
- I do not believe that there is evidence for a recent rise in global temperature (6)

Willingness to Accept Expert Recommendations

Using a scale from 0 to 6, how would you rate your willingness to accept the recommendations or information provided by a member of one of the following groups when they are advising within their area of expertise, where 0 indicates complete unwillingness and 6 equals complete willingness?

	Completely Unwilling 0 (0)	1 (1)	2 (2)	3 (3)	4 (4)	5 (5)	Completely Willing 6 (6)
Scientists (1)							
Medical doctors (2)							
Government officials (3)							
Business leaders (4)							
Religious leaders (5)							
Journalists (6)							
Lawyers (7)							
Scholars of history, philosophy, or English (8)							

Endorsement of Verifiable Facts

For the following questions, please select the choice that best answers the question. If you are unsure, please select your best estimate.

Over the past ten years, have violent crime rates in the U.S. generally been increasing or decreasing?[1]
- Increasing (1)
- Staying the same (2)
- Decreasing (3)*

---

[1] This item, included in the original scale, was later found out to be misleading, as recent trends have reversed. Hence, because of this lack of clarity, we have excluded it from our analyses.

Recent [scientific* / federal**][2] estimates suggest that [2,975* / 64**] people died in Puerto Rico as a result of Hurricane Maria. Do you think that this estimate is too high, approximately right, or too low?
- Too high (1)
- Approximately right (2)*
- Too low (3)**

Between 2008 and 2012, did U.S. drone strikes in Afghanistan kill more enemy combatants or innocent people?
- More enemy combatants (1)*
- About the same number of each (2)
- More innocent people (3)

At present, are there more Muslims or Jews living in the United States?
- More Muslims (1)
- About the same number of each (2)
- More Jews (3)*

Based on existing forecasts, in how many years will the size of the minority population in the United States surpass the size of the White population?
- 5–10 years (1)
- 11–20 years (2)
- 21–30 years (3)*

---

[2] Respondents were randomly assigned to one of two different wordings of this question (the asterisks indicate how the different versions fit together). This manipulation was conducted for exploratory purposes outside the scope of this study. For purposes of the study, these two versions were treated identically for scoring.

Rejection of False Conspiracy Theories

For each of the items below, please indicate how much you agree, using a scale of 0 to 5, where 0 indicates strongly disagree and 5 equals strongly agree.

The U.S. government caused or let the 9/11 attack happen on purpose.
- 0 Strongly disagree (0)
- 1 (1)
- 2 (2)
- 3 (3)
- 4 (4)
- 5 Strongly agree (5)
- Unsure (6)

Barack Obama was not born in the United States.
- 0 Strongly disagree (0)
- 1 (1)
- 2 (2)
- 3 (3)
- 4 (4)
- 5 Strongly agree (5)
- Unsure (6)

At least some moon landings didn't actually happen and were instead faked productions in Hollywood.
- 0 Strongly disagree (0)
- 1 (1)
- 2 (2)
- 3 (3)
- 4 (4)
- 5 Strongly agree (5)
- Unsure (6)

The assassination of John F. Kennedy was part of a larger conspiracy.
- 0 Strongly disagree (0)
- 1 (1)
- 2 (2)
- 3 (3)
- 4 (4)
- 5 Strongly agree (5)
- Unsure (6)

[Tupac/Elvis][3] is not actually dead, and is still seen periodically in the United States.
- 0 Strongly disagree (0)
- 1 (1)
- 2 (2)
- 3 (3)
- 4 (4)
- 5 Strongly agree (5)
- Unsure (6)

Philosophical Positivism Versus Skepticism

For each of the items below, please indicate how much you agree, using a scale of 0 to 5, where 0 indicates strongly disagree and 5 equals strongly agree.

When applicable, the scientific method is the best way we have for understanding the natural world.
- 0 Strongly disagree (0)
- 1 (1)
- 2 (2)
- 3 (3)
- 4 (4)
- 5 Strongly agree (5)
- Unsure (6)

---

[3] Respondents were randomly assigned to either the Elvis Presley or Tupac Shakur version of this question. This was conducted for exploratory purposes outside the scope of this study. For purposes of the study, the versions were treated identically for scoring.

There are objective standards for what is right and wrong.
- 0 Strongly disagree (0)
- 1 (1)
- 2 (2)
- 3 (3)
- 4 (4)
- 5 Strongly agree (5)
- Unsure (6)

Ability to Distinguish Fact from Opinion

[The following items were modified from a questionnaire fielded by the Pew Research Center (Mitchell et al., 2018).]

You will now be shown a series of statements that have been taken from news stories. Regardless of how knowledgeable you are about the topic, would you consider this statement to be a statement that could be verified using facts (regardless of whether you think it is accurate or not) OR a statement that relies on values or opinion (regardless of whether you agree with it or not)?

	Verifiable Using Facts (1)	Relies on Values or Opinion (2)
Immigrants who are in the U.S. illegally have some rights under the Constitution (1)	*	
Government is almost always wasteful and inefficient (2)		*
Spending on Social Security, Medicare, and Medicaid makes up the largest portion of the U.S. federal budget (3)	*	
Increasing the federal minimum wage to $15 an hour is essential for the health of the U.S. economy (4)		*
Immigrants who are in the U.S. illegally are a very big problem for the country today (5)		*
Health care costs per person in the U.S. are the highest in the developed world (6)	*	

Religious Affiliation and Service Attendance

Please choose the answer that best fits your religious affiliation.

What is your religion?
- Catholic (1)
- Orthodox Christian (2)
- Baptist (3)
- Methodist (4)
- Lutheran (5)
- Presbyterian (6)
- Episcopalian/Anglican (7)
- Evangelical Christian (8)
- Christian unspecified (9)
- Nondenominational Christian (10)
- Pentecostal (11)
- Mormon/Latter Day Saints (12)
- Jehovah's Witness (13)
- Seventh Day Adventist (14)
- Jewish (15)
- Muslim (16)
- Hindu (17)
- Buddhist (18)
- Other religion (19)
- No religion (20)
- Agnostic (21)
- Atheist (22)
- Don't know (23)

How often do you attend religious services?
- Never (1)
- Less than once a year (2)
- Once a year (3)
- Several times a year (4)
- Once a month (5)
- Two to three times a month (6)
- Nearly every week (7)
- Every week (8)
- More than once a week (9)

Scale Characteristics

Here we present details on the survey scales used in the analyses, including descriptive statistics and item-scale relationships.

Numeracy

Table B.1 shows performance on each of the eight numeracy items, which increase in difficulty as they progress. The numeracy index (Weller et al., 2013) was internally consistent (alpha = 0.72), similar to past studies.

TABLE B.1
Performance on the Eight Numeracy Items

Item	Proportion of Respondents That Answered Correctly	Item-Total Correlation (Excluding Item)
Disease percent	0.93	0.21
Disease frequency	0.87	0.38
Die rolls	0.72	0.39
Lottery	0.76	0.42
Sweepstakes	0.36	0.56
Ball and bat	0.18	0.44
Lily pads	0.37	0.55
Breast cancer	0.08	0.29

Scientific Reasoning

Table B.2 presents performance on the four items in the short-form Scientific Reasoning Scale. The four items on the short-form Scientific Reasoning Scale were also strongly intercorrelated, but the result was an only modestly internally consistent scale, likely because of the limited number of items (Cronbach alpha = 0.46). As noted, low reliability of this form can limit the ability to detect effects when used as a predictor.

Magical Reasoning

In line with prior studies of magical reasoning, we applied PCA to extract the axis that described the maximum variation on these items. Table B.3 shows the average and standard deviation of the responses to each item in the magical reasoning scale, along with the loadings of each on the first PC (PC1). The proportions of variation described by each component were

- PC1 = 0.34
- PC2 = 0.15
- PC3 = 0.12
- PC4 = 0.12
- PC5 = 0.10
- PC6 = 0.09
- PC7 = 0.08.

TABLE B.2
Performance on the Four Scientific Reasoning Items

Item	Proportion of Respondents That Answered Correctly	Item-Total Correlation (excluding item)
1. Confounding variables	0.79	0.20
2. Ecological validity	0.66	0.30
3. Maturation	0.57	0.28
4. Reliability	0.47	0.25

TABLE B.3
Summary of the Seven Magical Reasoning Items

Item	Average on 0–6 Disagree-to-Agree Scale	Standard Deviation	Loading on PC1
1. Have a sports superstition	1.3	1.7	0.28
2. Connections among events we don't understand	3.7	1.3	0.38
3. Uncomfortable buying a house in which a murder was committed	3.1	1.7	0.34
4. Act to avoid a jinx	2.2	1.6	0.42
5. Ancient people knew the universe's secrets	3.1	1.6	0.39
6. Things really happen for reason	3.9	1.3	0.43
7. Have sensed evil presence in a house	1.7	1.7	0.37

NOTE: PC1 loadings represent the first PC in an unrotated PCA with standardized scores.

Average responses for three items were on the "disagree" side of the scale (1, 4, and 7), but four items straddled the "unsure" category and had individuals who both agreed and disagreed with them. All the items load substantially and in the same direction on PC1. Cronbach's alpha for the seven magical reasoning items equaled 0.68.

Availability Bias

Table B.4 presents both descriptive statistics for the six availability bias questions, each scored for correctness (1 = correct; 0 = incorrect), and correlations among the items, as this instrument was newly created for this project. Items ranged substantially in difficulty with small-to-moderate positive correlations among the items. Two of the items (5 and 6) did not correlate as strongly with the other items, and as a result the internal consistency of an overall scale was low (alpha = 0.38).[1]

---

[1] We explored the potential for a shorter scale, using subsets of the items, but given the already low number of items, none of these alternatives substantially improved alpha.

TABLE B.4

Performance on the Six Availability Bias Items

Item	Proportion of Respondents That Answered Correctly	Item-Total Correlation (excluding item)
1. Attacked by sharks or killed by lightning	0.66	0.19
2. Struck by lightning or win the Powerball lottery	0.91	0.19
3. Suicide or homicide	0.58	0.23
4. Falls on stairs or storms	0.70	0.31
5. Physicians or post-secondary teachers	0.46	0.06
6. Motor vehicle accidents or poisoning	0.10	0.14

Ingroup Bias

In line with prior studies, we applied PCA to extract a single axis of greatest variation among the items (see Table B.5). The PCA of these binary items suggested that a single component was dominant over the others in terms of the percentage of total variance described, describing about twice the variation of the second component. Variances by PC were

- PC1 = 0.23
- PC2 = 0.13
- PC3 = 0.12
- PC4 = 0.10
- PC5 = 0.08
- PC6 = 0.08
- PC7 = 0.07
- PC8 = 0.07
- PC9 = 0.07
- PC10 = 0.06.

PC1 describes nearly twice the variance of the next component, PC2, and the gap between the variances described by PC1 and PC2 is the largest

TABLE B.5
Summary of the Ten Ingroup Bias Items

Item	Proportion "Would Not Mind" (versus "would not like") Out of All Responses	Loading on PC1
1. Drug addicts	0.05	0.08
2. Different race	0.98	0.37
3. People with AIDS	0.85	0.43
4. Immigrants	0.90	0.41
5. LGBT individuals	0.88	0.44
6. Different religion	0.98	0.24
7. Heavy drinkers	0.21	0.08
8. Unmarried couples	0.96	0.28
9. Different language	0.94	0.38
10. Different political views	0.93	0.17

NOTE: PC1 loadings represent the first PC in an unrotated PCA with standardized scores.

in the distribution which otherwise is a fairly gradual decline in variance described. Cronbach's alpha for the ingroup bias items equaled 0.55.

The summary statistics for ingroup bias show that most individuals "did not mind" having a neighbors of different demographics or different HIV or marital statuses, but "did not like" having heavy drinkers or drug dealers as neighbors. These latter two items also display comparatively weak loadings on PC1; most of the other variables load on PC1 at 0.25 or greater. We note that analyses of international samples have suggested all these items express a single underlying factor (Inglehart and Baker, 2000; Inglehart and Welzel, 2010; Ruck, Bentley, and Lawson, 2018; Ruck et al., 2019). Our results suggest that within an economically developed country, such as the United States, these items could load differently, with most loading together on an ethnocentrism–cosmopolitanism axis but attitudes about drugs and alcohol loading separately. This seems sensible—neighbors who use drugs and are heavy drinkers might expose individuals to materially negative effects on their own safety or just be a nuisance.

Endorsement of Scientific Consensus

Overall, the endorsement of scientific consensus scale was relatively internally consistent (alpha = 0.63), indicating that those who answered one question right also tended to answer other questions right (Table B.6).

Endorsement of Verifiable Facts

Overall, endorsement of verifiable facts was less internally consistent (alpha = 0.35), indicating that these five items might not strongly intercorrelate (Table B.7). Future work should examine refining this measure.

Rejection of False Conspiracy Theories

The tendency to reject such conspiracies was relatively consistent (alpha = 0.70) across items (Table B.8).

Willingness to Take Expert Recommendations

The willingness to take expert recommendations was also relatively consistent (alpha = 0.75) across items (Table B.9).

Ability to Distinguish Fact from Opinion

The ability to distinguish news items that relied primarily on fact versus opinion was relatively inconsistent (alpha = 0.32) (Table B.10).

Philosophical Positivism

We hypothesized that an additional aspect of the Truth Decay phenomenon could be a shift in public attitudes about whether ascertaining truth is at all objectively possible. We searched for published survey items to measure this stance toward truth (philosophical positivism versus skepticism); not finding any, we fielded two novel and exploratory questions related to this topic (Table B.11).

TABLE B.6

Performance on the Six Items Assessing Endorsement of Scientific Consensus

Item	Proportion Endorsing Scientific Consensus	Item-Total Correlation (excluding item)
1. Universe began with the Big Bang	0.45	0.54
2. Humans evolved from another species of animal	0.49	0.52
3. Safety of genetically modified food	0.33	0.33
4. Safety of vaccines	0.80	0.34
5. Homeopathic remedies are effective	0.40	0.23
6. Human activities have contributed to the rise in global temperature	0.70	0.26

TABLE B.7

Performance on the Five Items Assessing Endorsement of Verifiable Facts

Item	Proportion Correct	Item-Total Correlation (excluding item)
1. Number of illegal immigrants increasing or decreasing	0.27	0.24
3. Deaths in Puerto Rico resulting from Hurricane Maria	0.67	0.09
4. Drone strikes in Afghanistan kill more enemy combatants or innocent people	0.40	0.00
5. More Muslims or Jews in United States	0.43	0.25
6. When minority population in the United States will surpass White population	0.21	0.13

NOTE: An additional item #2 about trends in immigration was fielded but removed from the study because of concerns raised during review about this item's validity.

TABLE B.8

Performance on the Five Items Assessing Rejection of False Conspiracy Theories

Item	Mean	Item-Total Correlation (excluding item)
1. The U.S. government caused or let the 9/11 attack happen on purpose	1.14	0.49
2. Barack Obama was not born in the United States	1.43	0.35
3. At least some moon landings didn't actually happen and were instead faked productions in Hollywood	0.74	0.54
4. The assassination of John F. Kennedy was part of a larger conspiracy	2.53	0.49
5. [Tupac/Elvis] is not actually dead, and is still seen periodically in the United States	0.57	0.47

NOTE: Response options anchored such that 0 = strongly disagree, 3 = unsure, and 6 = strongly agree.

TABLE B.9

Performance on the Eight Items Assessing Willingness to Accept Recommendations or Information from Experts

Item	Mean	Item-Total Correlation (excluding item)
1. Scientists	4.30	0.45
2. Medical doctors	4.41	0.49
3. Government officials	2.45	0.57
4. Business leaders	2.98	0.46
5. Religious leaders	2.83	0.16
6. Journalists	2.63	0.52
7. Lawyers	2.97	0.55
8. Scholars of history, philosophy, or English	3.82	0.51

NOTE: Respondents were asked to "rate your willingness to accept the recommendations or information provided by a member of one of the following groups when they are advising within their area of expertise, where 0 indicates complete unwillingness and 6 equals complete willingness."

TABLE B.10

Performance on the Six Items Assessing Ability to Distinguish Fact from Opinion

Item	Proportion Correct	Item-Total Correlation (excluding item)
1. Immigrants who are in the United States illegally have some rights under the Constitution	0.71	0.15
2. Government is almost always wasteful and inefficient	0.54	0.21
3. Spending on Social Security, Medicare, and Medicaid makes up the largest portion of the U.S. federal budget	0.78	0.19
4. Increasing the federal minimum wage to $15 an hour is essential for the health of the U.S. economy	0.69	0.03
5. Immigrants who are in the United States illegally are a very big problem for the country today	0.65	0.16
6. Health care costs per person in the United States are the highest in the developed world	0.88	0.17

NOTE: Respondents were asked, "You will now be shown a series of statements that have been taken from news stories. Regardless of how knowledgeable you are about the topic, would you consider this statement to be a statement that could be verified using facts (regardless of whether you think it is accurate or not) OR a statement that relies on values or opinion (regardless of whether you agree with it or not)?"

TABLE B.11

Performance on the Two Items Assessing Philosophical Positivism Versus Skepticism

Item	Mean (0–5)	Correlation Between Two Items
1. When applicable, the scientific method is the best way we have for understanding the natural world.	3.69	0.16
2. There are objective standards for what is right and wrong.	3.48	

Methods

This appendix provides greater detail on key methodological elements of this study, notably the identification of our cognitive and Truth Decay measures, details of survey administration, and analytic approach.

Identifying Cognitive Biases Relevant to Truth Decay

Over at least the past 50 years, the study of human decisionmaking has identified a wide variety of cognitive processes that influence decisions along with biases that result from those processes (Gilovich, Griffin, and Kahneman, 2002; Kahneman, 2011). Truth Decay, at its root, is a set of phenomena regarding how people process and make judgments about information. Here we sought to canvass the broad set of identified biases, and the underlying processes that those biases imply, for those most likely to play a role in promoting (or mitigating) Truth Decay. The goal was to cast a broad net while prioritizing those biases that presented the greatest expected opportunity for impact, recognizing that in one project we could only address a fraction of the potential space of cognitive biases.

Identifying a Broad Universe of Potential Cognitive (and Social) Biases

Drawing on literature review, online searches, and expert judgment, we compiled a list of potential cognitive biases and cognitive processes. In doing so, we found no single authoritative list of such biases in the peer-reviewed literature. As a starting point, we drew heavily on an extensive online, crowdsourced list (Wikipedia, undated), augmented by our own knowledge of elements included and excluded from that list. Although not a formal literature review, this list has the advantage of reflecting the distributed knowledge of a wide variety of individuals and scholars. Entries come from many disciplines and often overlap; in the end, this encouraged us to expand our consideration beyond the purely "cognitive" to include biases with more social bases (for example, our inclusion of ingroup bias). We began by importing the list into an Excel database, organizing and combining clearly redundant entries; this resulted in a database of 186 potential biases.

Pile-Sort Methodology for Selecting Promising Candidates

We then leveraged the diverse disciplinary team makeup (anthropology, economics, psychology, political science) to conduct a rating and pile-sort exercise in which three researchers independently rated the 186 proposed biases or processes for relevance on a four-point scale and then sorted the 48 that were judged most relevant into conceptually related piles (Bernard, 1994). The 48 that were sorted were all judged by at least two researchers as possibly relevant to Truth Decay and potentially feasible to assess through a survey instrument. During the pile sort, four researchers independently made as many piles as they judged necessary to arrange the 48 relevant biases into conceptually similar groups. To conduct the pile sorts, the researchers used printed flashcards with the bias printed on one side and the definition on the other. We did this to reduce redundancies in the bias concepts and render them tractable to study within the confines of a ~20-minute survey. We did not specify in advance what these piles should be, and each researcher grouped the piles using their own organizing structure. The researchers then discussed their piles to (1) identify where consensus existed on piles and seek consensus where it did not already exist, (2) come to consensus on which biases belonged in which pile, and (3) identify piles, and biases within piles, that provided the best opportunities for measurement in a survey because existing published literature supported that they could be assessed through well-understood and validated tasks.

This process resulted in a final set of six cognitive biases and reasoning processes for inclusion in the survey: numeracy, scientific reasoning, magical reasoning, availability bias, unjustified confidence, and ingroup bias. Each bias or reasoning process required more than a single question to ensure robust measurement of it. We developed questions to measure the biases and reasoning processes through reference to prior survey studies that had measured them. Each is described in more detail, but, in total, 44 survey questions were deployed to measure the six biases and reasoning processes.

Results of the Card Sort Exercise

Using this approach, we identified three biases to focus on for this project, each hypothesized to be associated with greater Truth Decay and to be feasible to measure in our survey:

1. **Availability bias** (Tversky and Kahneman, 1974): Events that are easier to recall are also judged as more likely (the availability heuristic), which can cause likelihood judgments to be biased toward more salient or memorable events. For Truth Decay, distortion of risk perceptions should lead to argument and disbelief over objective risk information.

2. **Unjustified confidence** (Parker and Stone, 2014): An updated conceptualization of the older idea of overconfidence, this is confidence in knowledge (or perceived knowledge) that is unrelated to actual knowledge. A lack of understanding of the extent of one's own knowledge has the potential to limit information-seeking and increase rejection of expert judgment.

3. **Ingroup bias** (Newheiser et al., 2015; Wilkins-Laflamme, 2018; Inglehart and Baker, 2000): This bias is generally defined by a set of interrelated tendencies to feel more warmly toward one's cultural ingroup and to prefer them as partners during social interactions. This tendency, sometimes called ethnocentrism, appears to occur universally across modern societies (Langness, 1987), although its degree of expression is variable both across societies and among individuals within each society (Inglehart and Baker, 2000). What constitutes the ingroup varies, but often is defined by language, religion, ethnic background, nationality, or a combination of these features.

It should be noted that these do not represent the only biases deemed relevant to Truth Decay—merely those that best satisfied all the criteria. In particular, there were other prominent biases, such as confirmation bias (Klayman and Ha, 1987), that were clearly relevant to Truth Decay but were not, for example, easily administered in a short online survey.

During discussion of the biases, it also became apparent that there were several reasoning processes that could be associated with susceptibility to Truth Decay. By *reasoning process*, we mean a set of cognitive operations that work together according to a particular logic or domain of thought and that are more extensive in scope than a more singular bias that could be inserted within many cognitive pathways. Reasoning processes that were implicated in Truth Decay included

- **numeracy**, or skill with numbers, which has been shown to be a pervasive predictor of a wide variety of biases and decisionmaking behaviors (Peters, 2020; Weller et al., 2013)
- **scientific reasoning**, which extends the older concept of science literacy and has recently been identified as a potential driver of behaviors rejecting scientific consensus (for example, rejecting climate change and vaccine safety) (Drummond and Fischhoff, 2017; Drummond and Fischhoff, 2019)
- **magical reasoning**, which includes a variety of superstitious beliefs and at least conceptually represents a counterpoint to logical and scientific reasoning (Rosengren and French, 2013).

Drawing on this logic, we hypothesized that greater numeracy and scientific reasoning skill will be associated with lower resistance to Truth Decay, whereas greater magical reasoning will be associated with greater resistance to Truth Decay.

Identification and Development of Reasoning and Bias Indicators

Wherever possible, we capitalized on existing validated measures, which were more readily available for the reasoning constructs. When existing validated measures were not available, we developed new measures, taking lessons from existing approaches for assessing individual differences in cognitive biases (Bruine de Bruin, Parker, and Fischhoff, 2007; Stanovich, West, and Toplak, 2016). Verbatim question wording can be found in Appendix A.

Numeracy

We used a validated numeracy scale proposed by Weller et al. (2013), which builds off prior measures (for example, Lipkus, Samsa, and Rimer, 2001; Schwartz et al., 1997) but performs better across different ages and education levels. This eight-item measure assesses the ability of an individual to reason with numbers, with an emphasis on probabilistic reasoning. Each item is scored as correct or incorrect (with nonresponse scored as incorrect), and the overall score is the number of items scored as correct, from 0 to 8.

Scientific Reasoning

In consultation with the scale's first author, we used four items from the validated 11-item Scientific Reasoning Scale (Drummond and Fischhoff, 2017), which assesses the ability to evaluate scientific evidence in terms of the factors that determine its quality. Past research has shown that higher scores correlate positively with endorsement of scientific consensus on such issues as the safety of vaccines and genetically modified food, human evolution, and the Big Bang (Drummond and Fischhoff, 2017). As with numeracy, each item is scored as correct or incorrect (with nonresponse scored as incorrect), and the overall score is the number of items scored as correct, from 0 to 4.

Magical Reasoning

For magical reasoning, we adapted prior longer scales to create a new seven-item scale focused on the core features of magical reasoning that was informed by previous scales that used many more items (Eckblad and Chapman, 1983 [30 items]; Kingdon, Egan, and Rees, 2012 [27 items]). We adopted Rosengren and French's (2013) cross-cultural view of core components of magical reasoning to reduce and simplify the items from these longer instruments. Rosengren and French (2013) defined *magic* as "a belief in the existence of alternative forms of causality operating in the world, which works to bring about events that violate the normal causal order of the world." Magical reasoning is observed across numerous cultures, and often involves a supposition that highly similar objects share a hidden essence (magic by similarity), or that moral or spiritual acts create physical contamination and contagion (magic by contagion). An example of magic by similarity might include beliefs that photos of living or dead individuals can be used to connect with them spiritually; an example of magic by contagion would be avoidance of wearing clothing belonging to or being in a room occupied by a morally repugnant individual (for example, imagine wearing Adolf Hitler's sweater) (Rosengren and French, 2013). Magic also frequently invokes the notion that mental activity can alter physical reality, which is central to belief in jinxes and related superstitions (Kingdon, Egan, and Rees, 2012). Although both magic and religion involve beliefs in the supernatural, they are largely uncorrelated (Kingdon, Egan, and Rees, 2012), and it is theorized that this is because they serve different purposes to the believer. Magic practitioners and consumers seek to control unseen forces by compelling them with the aim of affecting observable reality by preventing bad luck, encouraging good luck, inducing romantic love, and so on. This is distinct from religion. Religion practitioners and consumers seek to supplicate unseen agents (gods) who can and do refuse supplications that mostly are oriented toward affecting a nonobservable reality, such as salvation in a future kingdom or afterlife (Stark, 2001). To operationalize magical reasoning, we created a new seven-item instrument with response options 0–5 that was based on previous but longer magical reasoning surveys.

Availability Bias

No standardized measure of availability bias existed prior to this study. To address this, we developed six items that asked respondents which of two events occurred more frequently. For example, one question asked, "In a typical year, are more people in the U.S. attacked by sharks or killed by lightning?" (More people are killed by lightning.) In each case, questions were designed such that respondents would be more likely to encounter information regarding the less frequent event, thus likely making it more available in memory (Tversky and Kahneman, 1974). Each item was scored as correct or incorrect, and a total score was computed as the percentage of correct responses out of all items responded to.

Confidence and Unjustified Confidence

Confidence in knowledge was assessed using an item referencing the eight-item numeracy scale, combined with the single law of small numbers item, asking respondents, "Considering the nine questions involving numbers that you just answered, how many do you think you got correct?"[1] Unjustified confidence is a relatively recently proposed alternative to the concept of *overconfidence* and is particularly useful as a predictor variable (Parker and Stone, 2014). Unjustified confidence is operationalized as the effect of confidence on a dependent variable (in this case, Truth Decay) after controlling for actual knowledge (here, numeracy plus the law of small numbers) (Parker and Stone, 2014).

Ingroup Bias

Ingroup bias was assessed using the standardized ten-item scale from the World Values Survey (Inglehart and Baker, 2000; Inglehart and Welzel, 2010). Respondents were prompted with, "On this list are various groups of people. Please indicate any that you would not like to have as neighbors." The list included

- drug addicts
- people of a different race
- people who have AIDS
- immigrants or foreign workers
- people who are lesbian, gay, bisexual, or transgender
- people of a different religion
- heavy drinkers
- unmarried couples living together
- people who speak a different language
- people of different political views.

Responses included "would not like" and "would not mind." Prior literature generally has assessed the intercorrelation of these items in cross-

---

[1] A second question, not used here, asked, "Considering the nine questions involving numbers that you just answered, what percent of ALP panelists do you think you scored better than?"

national data and found they load roughly equally on a single PC or factor (Inglehart and Baker, 2000; Inglehart and Welzel, 2010; Ruck, Bentley, and Lawson, 2018; Ruck et al., 2019). We replicated prior analyses of these items by applying PCA (with variables scaled) to the items and extracting the PC scores from the first component. That said, we hypothesized that specifically within an American sample, the items might not all load equally on a single component. By rerunning the analysis, we can examine whether the items do load equally, in which case we would replicate prior approaches; in the case they did not, we would extract a score more appropriate to the American sample than would be extracted by simply summing or averaging the items, which implicitly assumes they load equally.

Survey Administration and Analytic Approach

RAND American Life Panel and Selected Sample

The ALP consists of approximately 4,000 adults from across the United States. The ALP is a nationally representative panel that RAND has used since 2006 to track individual attitudes toward a variety of political and other issues. Panel members are recruited to the ALP using probability-based sampling methods (such as address-based sampling and random-digit dialing). Panel members agree to respond to regular online surveys, typically two to three per month. To ensure the representativeness of the panel, individuals who did not previously have access to the internet were provided with a netbook computer and internet access. A core set of demographic variables are regularly collected from all ALP panelists, with the most recent of these data automatically merged with data from each survey. This increases the efficiency for new surveys, which do not need to collect these data. [2]

For this study, we invited 1,626 ALP panelists, of whom 1,333 completed the survey (81.9-percent completion rate). Respondents for this survey were selected from a group who had previously participated in surveys con-

---

[2] Additional information about the ALP is available at the American Life Panel homepage (RAND Corporation, undated).

ducted during the 2016 presidential election and past surveys on vaccination, numeracy, or trust in institutions.

Weighting

Because all random samples will differ from the overall population that they
are selected to represent, the ALP generates sampling weights, which can be
applied to make the data as representative as possible. The ALP benchmarks
the weights against the Current Population Survey, using a raking procedure involving gender, age, race or ethnicity, education, number of household members, and household income. Additional details are available in
Pollard and Baird (2017).

Covariates

We considered a variety of socioeconomic and demographic variables along
with religiosity, political affiliation, and voting behavior. These include age
(treated linearly), gender (male or female), education (less than high school,
high school, some college, college degree), race or ethnicity (Hispanic, and
non-Hispanic White, Black, Asian, or other),[3] and whether the respondent
was born in the United States. Household income was collected via a set of
ranges (for example, $20,000 to $24,999), but was converted into a linear
variable for our regression analyses by taking the midpoint of the chosen
range and dividing that by 10,000, so that regression coefficients would display as a reasonable number of significant digits.

Treatment of Missing Data

Individual biases, reasoning measures, and Truth Decay indicators each were
assessed through multiple survey questions to ensure that the results were
robust to idiosyncrasies of interpretation of any single item. Generally, in
cases for which there is an objectively correct response, such as the scientific
or numerical reasoning questions, we treated a nonresponse as equivalent

---

[3] Throughout this analysis, we treated Hispanic as a category exclusive of other racial
groups. Individuals who identified as Hispanic were counted as this and not within any
other racial groups with which they identified.

to an incorrect response. In cases without an objectively correct response, we generally eliminated individuals if they did not answer any of the items. For some questions, such as the endorsement of false conspiracy theories, magical reasoning, and the philosophical positivism items, we were concerned that this might eliminate individuals who would not answer simply because they had never heard of, or thought about, the question. For those items, we offered a separate "unsure" radio button. We then assigned those unsure selections to the individual's own mean of the responses, within that set, for which the individual did not select "unsure." As a robustness check, we also considered assigning "unsure" as the midpoint of the response scale. The results were almost completely unaffected by this choice, so we present results using the individual's own mean.

Analytic Approach

We first describe the sample, both before and after applying weights, using simple means, standard deviations, and percentages. Then, because many of the measures presented here are newly constructed, we provide summary statistics and the Cronbach alpha for each scale. Alpha (reported in Appendix B) assesses the degree to which items in a scale intercorrelate positively, as would be expected if they all reflect the same underlying construct. It is often taken as an indicator for internal consistency. It ranges from 0 to 1; higher scores indicate greater internal consistency. Traditionally, scores of 0.70 or higher are desired, but lower scores are acceptable for early stages of predictive or construct validity research (Nunnally and Bernstein, 1994). In practice, lower measurement reliability limits the ability to detect true relationships with other variables (essentially, it is harder to distinguish the signal from the noise).

We next examine bivariate relationships among our variables of interest, both within and between variable sets. Finally, to test our main hypothesis that resistance to Truth Decay is associated with less rigorous reasoning and greater cognitive bias, we conducted three sets of regression analyses. The first predicts each of our proposed measures of resistance to Truth Decay with our measures of reasoning and bias while controlling for the covariates already described.

The second approach accounts for the possibility that our a priori grouping of survey items into scales of resistance/susceptibility to Truth Decay (for example, conspiracy theories, verifiable facts) does not reflect how Americans think about these issues. It is possible that we, as researchers, come to the table with our own misconceptions about how aspects of Truth Decay are organized. For example, although we have proposed that conspiracy theories and nonconspiratorial verifiable facts are distinct scales, it is an empirical question whether these scales are distinct cognitively in most people's minds. To analyze the data in a manner agnostic to our own grouping of survey items, we subject the entire pool of individual Truth Decay items to PCA (with standardized scores and no rotation) and extract component scores for each individual respondent on each of the major components identified. These component scores are then treated, similar to the a priori scales of resistance/susceptibility to Truth Decay, as outcome variables in regression models with reasoning, biases, and our covariates as predictors.

The third approach adopts an even more relativist stance than the second. In the second approach, we relax our own assumptions about how Truth Decay items fit into categories; in the third approach, we relax our assumptions about which answers to each Truth Decay item are the "truth" versus the "decay." Both approaches just discussed have the individual items oriented from one end (which external scholarly standards generally indicate as truth) and the other end (thought of as Truth Decay). We can instead consider whether individuals deviate from the "consensus truth" about these items, defined as whatever the majority of the respondents themselves answered. This culturally relative notion is based on the conception that *truth* is a body of agreed beliefs shared by a society (Romney, Batchelder, and Weller, 1987; Romney, Weller, and Batchelder, 1986; Weller, 2007). Anthropologists working in cross-cultural settings developed CCA as a robust method for measuring each individual's relative agreement with the central tendency across all individuals and across all survey items. This method works by applying PCA to the transpose of the matrix of individuals (rows) by beliefs (columns) analyzed in the first two approaches described. In essence, this analysis focuses on covariation of people across beliefs rather than of beliefs across people. The loading of each individual on the first component of this analysis reflects the level of agreement that an individual has with the central tendency of responses from all individuals, across all survey items. We first validate this output against standard benchmarks for CCA (essentially ensuring a dominant first PC), then proceed to use the CCA loadings for each individual as an outcome variable in a regression model with reasoning, biases, and our covariates as predictors. This outcome variable reflects how close an individual's beliefs are to the average or most prototypical beliefs within the culture.

Consensus Analysis Implementation with a Formal Model for Chance Answers

Table C.1 shows results for the "formal" implementation of CCA through the UCINET software. The comparison of these results to the "informal" implementation, which we think is more appropriate to these data, is discussed in the main text.

TABLE C.1
Truth Decay Models from UCINET CCA

Characteristic	Principle Component Outcome Models
	UCINET CCA
Age	−0.002
Female	0.16[**]
Education	
Less than high school	−0.32
Some college	0.16
College degree	0.12
Income midpoint/10,000	0.01
Race	
Hispanic ($n = 148$)	−0.16
Black, non-Hispanic ($n = 81$)	−0.28[**]
Asian, non-Hispanic ($n = 33$)	0.04
Other, non-Hispanic ($n = 26$)	−0.2
Born in United States	−0.01

Table C.1—Continued

Characteristic	Principle Component Outcome Models
	CCA UCINET
Religion	
Mainstream Protestant	−0.03
Evangelical or Pentecostal	−0.22
Nondenominational Christian	−0.05
Other Christian groups	−0.09
Jewish	0.24
Other religions	−0.15
No religious affiliation	0.11
Atheist or agnostic	0.03
Religious service attendance	−0.02
Political affiliation	
Democrat	−0.12
Republican	−0.06
Clinton voter in 2016	−0.03
Trump voter in 2016	−0.07
Measures of reasoning or cognitive bias	
Numeracy	0.01
Scientific reasoning	−0.02
Magical reasoning	0.05**
Availability bias	−0.16
Unjustified confidence	−0.03
Ingroup bias	0.19***
Constant	2.60***
Observations	1,291
R^2	0.13
Adjusted R^2	0.11
Residual SE	0.79 (df = 1259)
F statistic	6.18*** (df = 31; 1259)

NOTES: Base levels: male, high school, non-Hispanic White, born outside United States, Catholic, independent political affiliation, voted for other candidate in 2016. Responses of "unsure" have been assigned a random value from across that single item's distribution. $* p < 0.05$; $** p < 0.01$; $*** p < 0.001$.

Abbreviations

9/11	September 11, 2001, attacks
ALP	RAND American Life Panel
CART	Comprehensive Assessment of Rational Thinking
CCA	Cultural Consensus Analysis
df	degree of freedom
PC	principal component
PCA	principal component analysis
SD	standard deviation
SE	standard error

References

Alba, Joseph W., and J. Wesley Hutchinson, "Knowledge Calibration: What Consumers Know and What They Think They Know," *Journal of Consumer Research*, Vol. 27, No. 2, 2000, pp. 123–156.

Alesina, Alberto, Edward Glaeser, and Bruce Sacerdote, "Why Doesn't the United States Have a European-Style Welfare State?" *Brookings Papers on Economic Activity*, No. 2, 2001, pp. 1–69.

Bernard, H. Russell, *Research Methods in Anthropology: Qualitative and Quantitative Approaches*, Lanham, Md.: Rowman Altamira, 1994.

Bernard, H. Russell, *Research Methods in Anthropology: Qualitative and Quantitative Approaches*, 6th ed., Lanham, Md.: Rowman & Littlefield, 2018.

Bogart, Laura M., Lu Dong, Priya Gandhi, David J. Klein, Terry L. Smith, Samantha Ryan, and Bisola O. Ojikutu, "COVID-19 Vaccine Intentions and Mistrust in a National Sample of Black Americans," *Journal of the National Medical Association*, June 2021.

Borgatti, Stephen P., Martin G. Everett, and Linton C. Freeman, *Ucinet 6 for Windows: Software for Social Network Analysis*, Cambridge, Mass.: Analytic Technologies, 2002.

Boyd, Robert, and Peter J. Richerson, *Culture and the Evolutionary Process*, Chicago, Ill.: University of Chicago Press, 1985.

Brotherton, Robert, and Christopher C. French, "Belief in Conspiracy Theories and Susceptibility to the Conjunction Fallacy," *Applied Cognitive Psychology*, Vol. 28, No. 2, 2014, pp. 238–248.

Bruine de Bruin, Wändi, Andrew M. Parker, and Baruch Fischhoff, "Individual Differences in Adult Decision-Making Competence," *Journal of Personality and Social Psychology*, Vol. 92, No. 5, 2007, pp. 938–956.

Brunson, Emily K., and Elisa J. Sobo, "Framing Childhood Vaccination in the United States: Getting Past Polarization in the Public Discourse," *Human Organization*, Vol. 76, No. 1, 2017, pp. 38–47.

Butterfield, Herbert, *The Origins of Modern Science*, New York: The Free Press, 1957.

Celious, Aaron, and Daphna Oyserman, "Race from the Inside: An Emerging Heterogeneous Race Model," *Journal of Social Issues*, Vol. 57, No. 1, 2001, pp. 149–165.

Clark, Cory J., and Philip E. Tetlock, "Adversarial Collaboration: The Next Science Reform," in C. L. Frisby, R. E. Redding, W. T. O'Donohue, and S. O. Lilienfeld, eds., *Political Bias in Psychology: Nature, Scope, and Solutions*, New York: Springer, 2022.

Combs, Barbara, and Paul Slovic, "Newspaper Coverage of Causes of Death," *Journalism Quarterly*, Vol. 56, No. 4, December 1979, pp. 837–849.

Davies, Brian, "Series Foreword: Great Medieval Thinkers," in Deirdre Carabine, ed., *John Scottus Eriugena*, New York: Oxford University Press, 2000.

Drouhot, Lucas G., and Filiz Garip, "What's Behind a Racial Category? Uncovering Heterogeneity Among Asian Americans Through a Data-Driven Typology," *RSF: The Russel Sage Foundation Journal of the Social Sciences*, Vol. 7, No. 2, 2021, pp. 22–45.

Drummond, Caitlin, and Baruch Fischhoff, "Development and Validation of the Scientific Reasoning Scale," *Journal of Behavioral Decision Making*, Vol. 30, No. 1, 2017, pp. 26–38.

Drummond, Caitlin, and Baruch Fischhoff, "Does 'Putting on Your Thinking Cap' Reduce Myside Bias in Evaluation of Scientific Evidence?" *Thinking & Reasoning*, Vol. 25, No. 4, 2019, pp. 477–505.

Eckblad, Mark, and Loren J. Chapman, "Magical Ideation as an Indicator of Schizotypy," *Journal of Consulting and Clinical Psychology*, Vol. 51, No. 2, 1983, pp. 215–225.

Gidengil, Courtney, Christine Chen, Andrew M. Parker, Sarah Nowak, and Luke Matthews, "Beliefs Around Childhood Vaccines in the United States: A Systematic Review," *Vaccine*, Vol. 37, No. 45, 2019, pp. 6793–6802.

Gilovich, Thomas, Dale Griffin, and Daniel Kahneman, eds., *Heuristics and Biases: The Psychology of Intuitive Judgment*, Cambridge, UK: Cambridge University Press, 2002.

Haselton, Martie G., David Nettle, and Damian R. Murray, "The Evolution of Cognitive Bias," in David M. Buss, ed., *The Handbook of Evolutionary Psychology*, Hoboken, N.J.: John Wiley & Sons, 2016.

Inglehart, Ronald, and Wayne E. Baker, "Modernization, Cultural Change, and the Persistence of Traditional Values," *American Sociological Review*, Vol. 65, No. 1, 2000, pp. 19–51.

Inglehart, Ronald, and Christian Welzel, "Changing Mass Priorities: The Link Between Modernization and Democracy," *Perspective on Politics*, Vol. 8, No. 2, 2010, pp. 551–567.

Jolliffe, I. T., *Principal Component Analysis*, New York: Springer, 2003.

Kahne, Joseph, and Benjamin Bowyer, "Educating for Democracy in a Partisan Age: Confronting the Challenges of Motivated Reasoning and Misinformation," *American Educational Research Journal*, Vol. 54, No. 1, 2018, pp. 3–34.

Kahneman, Daniel, *Thinking, Fast and Slow*, New York: Macmillan, 2011.

Kavanagh, Jennifer, and Michael D. Rich, *Truth Decay: An Initial Exploration of the Diminishing Role of Facts and Analysis in American Public Life*, Santa Monica, Calif.: RAND Corporation, RR-2314-RC, 2018. As of November 19, 2021:
https://www.rand.org/pubs/research_reports/RR2314.html

Kennedy, Courtney, Nick Hatley, Arnold Lau, Andrew Mercer, Scott Keeter, Joshua Ferno, and Dorene Asare-Marfo, *Assessing the Risks to Online Polls from Bogus Respondents*, Washington, D.C.: Pew Research Center, 2020.

Kingdon, Bianca L., Sarah J. Egan, and Clare S. Rees, "The Illusory Beliefs Inventory: A New Measure of Magical Thinking and Its Relationship with Obsessive Compulsive Disorder," *Behavioural and Cognitive Psychotherapy*, Vol. 40, No. 1, 2012, pp. 39–53.

Klayman, Joshua, and Young-Won Ha, "Confirmation, Disconfirmation, and Information in Hypothesis Testing," *Psychological Review*, Vol. 94, No. 2, 1987.

Langness, L. L., *The Study of Culture*, Novato, Calif.: Chandler Sharp, 1987.

Levin, Irwin P., Sandra L. Schneider, and Gary J. Gaeth, "All Frames Are Not Created Equal: A Typology and Critical Analysis of Framing Effects," *Organizational Behavior and Human Decision Processes*, Vol. 76, 1998, pp. 149–188.

Lewandowsky, Stephan, Gilles E. Gignac, and Klaus Oberauer, "The Role of Conspiracist Ideation and Worldviews in Predicting Rejection of Science," *PLOS ONE*, Vol. 8, No. 10, 2013.

Lipkus, Isaac M., Greg Samsa, and Barbara K. Rimer, "General Performance on a Numeracy Scale Among Highly Educated Samples," *Medical Decision Making*, Vol. 21, No. 1, 2001, pp. 37–44.

Matthews, Luke J., Ryan Andrew Brown, and David P. Kennedy, *A Manual for Cultural Analysis*, Santa Monica, Calif.: RAND Corporation, TL-275, 2018. As of December 28, 2021:
https://www.rand.org/pubs/tools/TL275.html

Matthews, Luke J., Sarah Nowak, Courtney Gidengil, Christine Chen, Joseph M. Stubbersfield, Jamshid J. Tehrani, and Andrew M. Parker, "Belief Correlations with Parental Vaccine Hesitancy: Results from a National Survey," *American Anthropologist*, 2022.

Mitchell, Amy, Jeffrey Gottfried, Michael Barthel, and Nami Sumida, "Distinguishing Between Factual and Opinion Statements in the News," Pew Research Center, June 18, 2018.

Nelson, Wendy, Valerie F. Reyna, Angela Fagerlin, Isaac Lipkus, and Ellen Peters, "Clinical Implications of Numeracy: Theory and Practice," *Annals of Behavioral Medicine*, Vol. 35, No. 3, 2008, pp. 261–274.

Newheiser, Anna-Kaisa, Miles Hewstone, Alberto Voci, and Katharina Schmid, "Making and Unmaking Prejudice: Religious Affiliation Mitigates the Impact of Mortality Salience on Out-Group Attitudes," *Journal for the Scientific Study of Religion*, Vol. 54, No. 4, 2015, pp. 774–791.

Nowak, Sarah A., Christine Chen, Andrew M. Parker, Courtney A. Gidengil, and Luke J. Matthews, "Comparing Covariation Among Vaccine Hesitancy and Broader Beliefs Within Twitter and Survey Data," *PLOS ONE*, October 8, 2020.

Nunnally, Jum C., and Ira H. Bernstein, *Psychometric Theory*, 3rd ed., New York: McGraw-Hill, 1994.

Nyhan, Brendan, Jason Reifler, Sean Richey, and Gary L. Freed, "Effective Messages in Vaccine Promotion: A Randomized Trial," *Pediatrics*, Vol. 133, No. 4, 2014.

Opel, Douglas J., Nora Henrikson, Katherine Lepere, Rene Hawkes, Chuan Zhou, John Dunn, and James A. Taylor, "Previsit Screening for Parental Vaccine Hesitancy: A Cluster Randomized Trial," *Pediatrics*, Vol. 144, No. 5, 2019.

Parker, Andrew M., Wändi Bruine de Bruin, and Baruch Fischhoff, "Negative Decision Outcomes Are More Common Among People with Lower Decision-Making Competence: An Item-Level Analysis of the Decision Outcome Inventory (DOI)," *Frontiers of Psychology, Cognition*, Vol. 6, Article 363, 2015, pp. 1–7.

Parker, Andrew M., Wändi Bruine de Bruin, Baruch Fischhoff, and Joshua Weller, "Robustness of Decision-Making Competence: Evidence from Two Measures and an 11-Year Longitudinal Study," *Journal of Behavioral Decision Making*, Vol. 31, No. 3, 2018, pp. 380–391.

Parker, Andrew M., and Eric R. Stone, "Identifying the Effects of Unjustified Confidence Versus Overconfidence: Lessons Learned from Two Analytic Methods," *Journal of Behavioral Decision Making*, Vol. 27, No. 2, 2014, pp. 134–145.

Peters, Ellen, *Innumeracy in the Wild: Misunderstanding and Misusing Numbers*, New York: Oxford University Press, 2020.

Pollard, Michael, and Matthew Baird, *The RAND American Life Panel: Technical Description*, Santa Monica, Calif.: RAND Corporation, RR-1651, 2017. As August 24, 2020:
https://www.rand.org/pubs/research_reports/RR1651.html

RAND Corporation, American Life Panel, homepage, undated. As of December 28, 2021:
https://alpdata.rand.org/

Reeves, Richard V., and Eleanor Krause, "Raj Chetty in 14 Charts: Big Findings on Opportunity and Mobility We Should All Know," *Social Mobility Memo*, Brookings Institution, January 11, 2018.

Reyna, Valerie F., "A Theory of Medical Decision Making and Health: Fuzzy Trace Theory," *Medical Decision Making*, Vol. 28, No. 6, 2008, pp. 850–865.

Romney, A. Kimball, William H. Batchelder, and Susan C. Weller, "Recent Applications of Cultural Consensus," *American Behavioral Scientist*, Vol. 31, No. 2, 1987, pp. 163–177.

Romney, A. Kimball, Susan C. Weller, and William H. Batchelder, "Culture and Consensus: A Theory of Culture and Informant Accuracy," *American Anthropologist*, Vol. 88, No. 2, 1986, pp. 313–338.

Rosengren, Karl S., and Jason A. French, "Magical Thinking," in Marjorie Taylor, ed., *Oxford Library of Psychology. The Oxford Handbook of the Development of Imagination*, Oxford University Press, 2013, pp. 42–60.

Ruck, Damian J., R. Alexander Bentley, and Daniel J. Lawson, "Religious Change Preceded Economic Change in the 20th Century," *Science Advances*, Vol. 4, No. 7, 2018.

Ruck, Damian J., Luke J. Matthews, Thanos Kyritsis, Quentin D. Atkinson, and R. Alexander Bentley, "The Cultural Foundations of Modern Democracies," *Nature Human Behaviour*, Vol. 4, No. 3, 2019, pp. 265–269.

Scheufele, Dietram A., and Nicole M. Krause, "Science Audiences, Misinformation, and Fake News," *Proceedings of the National Academy of Sciences*, Vol. 116, No. 16, 2019, pp. 7662–7669.

Schwartz, Lisa M., Steven Woloshin, William C. Black, and H. Gilbert Welch, "The Role of Numeracy in Understanding the Benefit of Screening Mammography," *Annals of Internal Medicine*, Vol. 127, No. 11, 1997, pp. 966–972.

Stanovich, Keith, *Rationality and the Reflective Mind*, New York: Oxford University Press, 2011.

Stanovich, Keith E., and Richard F. West, "Individual Differences in Reasoning: Implications for the Rationality Debate?" *Behavioral and Brain Sciences*, Vol. 23, No. 5, 2000, pp. 645–665.

Stanovich, Keith E., Richard F. West, and Maggie E. Toplak, "Myside Bias, Rational Thinking, and Intelligence," *Current Directions in Psychological Science*, Vol. 22, No. 4, 2013, pp. 259–264.

Stanovich, Keith E., Richard F. West, and Maggie E. Toplak, *The Rationality Quotient: Toward a Test of Rational Thinking*, Cambridge Mass.: MIT Press, 2016.

Stark, Rodney, "Reconceptualizing Religion, Magic, and Science," *Review of Religious Research,* Vol. 43, No. 2, December 2001, pp. 101–120.

Tversky, Amos, and Daniel Kahneman, "Judgment Under Uncertainty: Heuristics and Biases," *Science*, Vol. 185, No. 4157, 1974, pp. 1124–1131.

Uscinski, Joseph E., and Joseph M. Parent, *American Conspiracy Theories*, New York: Oxford University Press, 2014.

Vanderbilt University, "AmericasBarometer 2018/19," webpage, undated. As of February 1, 2019:
https://www.vanderbilt.edu/lapop/ab2018.php

Waubert de Puiseau, Berenike, André Aßfalg, Edgar Erdfelder, and Daniel M. Bernstein, "Extracting the Truth from Conflicting Eyewitness Reports: A Formal Modeling Approach," *Journal of Experimental Psychology: Applied,* Vol. 18, No. 4, 2012, pp. 390–403.

Weller, Joshua A., Nathan F. Dieckmann, Martin Tusler, C. K. Mertz, William J. Burns, and Ellen Peters, "Development and Testing of an Abbreviated Numeracy Scale: A Rasch Analysis Approach," *Journal of Behavioral Decision Making*, Vol. 26, No. 2, 2013, pp. 198–212.

Weller, Susan C., "Cultural Consensus Theory: Applications and Frequently Asked Questions," *Field Methods*, Vol. 19, 2007, pp. 339–368.

Westergaard, Ryan P., Mary Catherine Beach, Somnath Saha, and Elizabeth A. Jacobs, "Racial/Ethnic Differences in Trust in Health Care: HIV Conspiracy Beliefs and Vaccine Research Participation," *Journal of General Internal Medicine*, Vol. 29, No. 1, 2014, pp. 140–146.

Wilkins-Laflamme, Sarah, "Islamophobia in Canada: Measuring the Realities of Negative Attitudes Toward Muslims and Religious Discrimination," *Canadian Review of Sociology*, Vol. 55, No. 1, 2018, pp. 86–110.

Wikipedia, "List of Cognitive Biases," undated. As of February 1, 2019:
https://en.wikipedia.org/wiki/List_of_cognitive_biases

Lightning Source UK Ltd.
Milton Keynes UK
UKHW020614150622
404459UK00005B/105